VITAL GREENS

80 POWER-PACKED SMOOTHIE RECIPES FOR RAPID WEIGHT LOSS AND DEEP CLEANSING

JASMINE PATEL

2023

TABLE OF CONTENTS

INTRODUCTION _____ 6
WHY ARE GREEN SMOOTHIES GOOD FOR YOUR HEALTH? _____ 7
HOW BLENDING OUTPERFORMS JUICING FOR YOUR HEALTH __ 8
HOW TO CHOOSE A BLENDER FOR MAKING GREEN SMOOTHIES
_____ 10
BONUS TIPS _____ 12
RECIPES _____ 13

RASPBERRY BANANA GREEN SMOOTHIE _____ 13

STRAWBERRY BANANA GREEN SMOOTHIE _____ 14

CELERY APPLE AND KIWI SMOOTHIE _____ 15

PINEAPPLE MINT SMOOTHIE WITH PISTACHIOS _____ 16

CHERRY VANILLA GREEN SMOOTHIE _____ 17

MANGO BANANA GREEN SMOOTHIE _____ 18

PINEAPPLE COCONUT GREEN SMOOTHIE _____ 19

PEACH MANGO GREEN SMOOTHIE _____ 20

RASPBERRY PINEAPPLE GREEN SMOOTHIE _____ 21

ORANGE CARROT GREEN SMOOTHIE _____ 22

APPLE BERRY GREEN SMOOTHIE _____ 23

BERRY PEACHY GREEN SMOOTHIE _____ 24

SPINACH KALE BERRY SMOOTHIE _____ 25

PEACH BANANA GREEN SMOOTHIE _____ 26

WATERMELON GINGER GREEN SMOOTHIE _____ 27

BANANA CHIA GREEN SMOOTHIE _____ 28

CHERRY WHEATGRASS GREEN SMOOTHIE _____ 29

BERRY PROTEIN GREEN SMOOTHIE	30
BERRY SEEDS SPINACH GREEN SMOOTHIE	31
NUT CELERY PROTEIN GREEN SMOOTHIE	32
MANGO MATCHA GREEN SMOOTHIE	33
GREEN SPIRULINA SMOOTHIE	34
COLD BUSTER CITRUS GREEN SMOOTHIE	35
BERRY PUMPKIN PROTEIN GREEN SMOOTHIE	35
PAPAYA LEMON GREEN SMOOTHIE	37
MULTIFRUIT GREEN SMOOTHIE	38
CUCUMBER STRAWBERRY GREEN SMOOTHIE	39
BANANA NUT GREEN SMOOTHIE	40
VANILLA-MINT GREEN SMOOTHIE	41
TROPICAL GREEN SMOOTHIE	42
BASIL CANTALOUPE GREEN SMOOTHIE	43
BANANA BLUEBERRY GOOSEBERRY GREEN SMOOTHIE	44
ORANGE AVOCADO GREEN SMOOTHIE	45
COCONUT OIL DETOX GREEN SMOOTHIE	46
BROCCOLI GREEN SMOOTHIE	47
GINGER PEAR GREEN SMOOTHIE	48
BANANA PRUNE GREEN SMOOTHIE	49
ORANGE MANGO GREEN SMOOTHIE	50
GRAPEFRUIT BANANA GREEN SMOOTHIE	51
ORANGE BERRY SEEDS SMOOTHIE	53

MINTY PEAR GREEN SMOOTHIE	54
PEACHY MANGO GREEN SMOOTHIE	55
COCONUT BERRIES GREEN SMOOTHIE	56
SUNFLOWER ORANGE GREEN SMOOTHIE	57
AVOCADO APPLE SMOOTHIE	58
ORANGE APRICOT GREEN SMOOTHIE	59
CHOCOLATEY AND NUTTY GREEN SMOOTHIE	60
BERRY MEDLEY GREEN SMOOTHIE	61
CELERY AVOCADO GREEN SMOOTHIE	62
GREEN SMOOTHIE WITH CELERY CUCUMBER SPINACH	63
CELERY APPLE DETOX GREEN SMOOTHIE	64
GREEN SMOOTHIE WITH CELERY AND PARSLEY	65
AVOCADO CABBAGE SPINACH GREEN SMOOTHIE	66
PEANUT BUTTER-STRAWBERRY-KALE SMOOTHIE	67
PINEAPPLE-GRAPEFRUIT DETOX SMOOTHIE	68
ALOE SMOOTHIE	69
GREEN PIÑA COLADA SMOOTHIE	70
CREAMY ZUCCHINI SMOOTHIE	71
GREEN GRAPES SMOOTHIE	72
SUPER HEALTHY SMOOTHIE	73
GREEN SMOOTHIE WITH OATMEAL AND FLAX	74
LETTUCE AND GINGER DETOX SMOOTHIE	75
KALE AND GINGER GREEN SMOOTHIE	76

ARUGULA AND CUCUMBER SMOOTHIE	77
DANDELION AND WATERCRESS SMOOTHIE	77
LETTUCE AND ORANGE SMOOTHIE	79
BERRIES AND HEMP SEEDS SMOOTHIE	80
PEAR, BERRIES, AND QUINOA SMOOTHIE	81
BERRIES AND SEA MOSS SMOOTHIE	82
RASPBERRY AND CHARD SMOOTHIE	83
BANANA, BERRY, AND KALE SMOOTHIE	84
CUCUMBER AND COCONUT SMOOTHIE	85
SAGE BLACKBERRY SMOOTHIE	86
STRAWBERRY LIME SMOOTHIE	87
FRESH PURPLE FIG SMOOTHIE	88
STRAWBERRY BEET SMOOTHIE	89
ZUCCHINI, WATERMELON AND COCONUT OIL SMOOTHIE	90
CUCUMBER, PLAME AND CUMIN SMOOTHIE	91
LEAVES OF THE AMARANTH, STRAWBERRY AND SWEET BASIL SMOOTHIE	92

MAIN INGREDIENTS USED AND ITS BENEFITS 93
CONCLUSION 96

INTRODUCTION

Welcome to the world of green smoothies - a delicious and healthy way to start your day! In this recipe book, you will find 80 green smoothie recipes that will leave you feeling energized, refreshed, and ready to take on the day.

Green smoothies are a powerful way to get your daily dose of vitamins and minerals, and they are an excellent source of fiber, protein, and antioxidants. They are also an easy way to incorporate leafy greens and other nutrient-rich foods into your diet, even if you're not a fan of eating them in their natural state.

The beauty of green smoothies is that they can be tailored to your individual tastes and preferences. Whether you like your smoothies sweet or savory, fruity or nutty, this book has something for everyone. Each recipe has been carefully crafted to ensure that it not only tastes great but is also packed with the nutrients your body needs to thrive.

One of the many benefits of green smoothies is their versatility. They can be enjoyed as a quick breakfast on-the-go, a mid-day snack, or even as a post-workout pick-me-up. They are also an excellent way to stay hydrated throughout the day, especially during the hot summer months.

In this book, you will find recipes for classic green smoothies, such as spinach and kale, as well as more unique combinations that incorporate ingredients like avocado, ginger, and even matcha green tea. You'll learn how to create smoothies that are creamy, fruity, and refreshing, as well as those that are packed with protein and healthy fats.

I know that eating healthy can sometimes feel overwhelming, especially when you're short on time. That's why each recipe in this book is designed to be quick and easy to make, with minimal prep work required. All you need is a blender, some fresh ingredients, and a few minutes, and you'll be on your way to enjoying a delicious and nutritious green smoothie.

So why not give green smoothies a try? Your body will thank you for it. I hope that this recipe book will inspire you to incorporate more plant-based foods into your diet and help you discover the many benefits of green smoothies. Get ready to feel energized, nourished, and satisfied with every sip!

WHY ARE GREEN SMOOTHIES GOOD FOR YOUR HEALTH?

Green smoothies are a popular drink choice among health enthusiasts, and for good reason. Not only are they delicious, but they are also incredibly nutritious. The addition of leafy greens, vegetables, and fruits makes for a tasty and vitamin-packed drink that can boost your health in numerous ways.

One of the primary benefits of green smoothies is their ability to provide a wide variety of nutrients in a single drink. By blending a variety of greens, fruits, and vegetables together, you can get an array of vitamins, minerals, and antioxidants that your body needs to function at its best. These nutrients can help to boost your immune system, improve your digestion, and provide you with sustained energy throughout the day.

In particular, the leafy greens that are commonly used in green smoothies are incredibly beneficial for your health. Greens like kale, spinach, and collard greens are rich in vitamins A, C, and K, as well as calcium, iron, and potassium. These nutrients can help to support healthy bones, boost your metabolism, and even reduce your risk of chronic diseases like heart disease and cancer.

Another benefit of green smoothies is their ability to help you maintain a healthy weight. By adding fruits and vegetables to your diet, you can increase your fiber intake, which can help you feel fuller for longer periods of time. This can lead to a reduction in overall calorie intake, which can help you lose weight or maintain a healthy weight.

Green smoothies are also a great way to stay hydrated. Many people struggle to drink enough water throughout the day, but by adding water-rich fruits and vegetables to your smoothie, you can help to keep your body hydrated and functioning at its best.

Finally, green smoothies are incredibly versatile and can be customized to your individual taste preferences. Whether you prefer sweet or savory flavors, there is a green smoothie recipe out there for you. You can add ingredients like nuts, seeds, and protein powder to your smoothie to make it more filling and satisfying, or you can add spices like ginger and turmeric for an added nutritional boost.

In conclusion, green smoothies are a delicious and nutritious drink that can benefit your health in numerous ways. From providing a wide range of essential nutrients to helping you maintain a healthy weight, adding green smoothies to your diet is a great way to support your overall health and wellbeing.

HOW BLENDING OUTPERFORMS JUICING FOR YOUR HEALTH

When it comes to juicing and blending, both methods have their health benefits, but blending is the superior option in many cases. Smoothies offer a more comprehensive range of benefits than juices since they contain more fiber, are more filling, and are less expensive and time-consuming to make.

One of the main advantages of blending is that it retains the whole food, including the pulp, which is rich in fiber. In contrast, juicing discards the pulp, leading to a loss of essential fiber. While juicing proponents argue that fiber-free nutrients are absorbed quickly into the bloodstream, fiber is crucial in slowing down food passage through the stomach, preventing quick sugar absorption and helping regulate blood sugar levels. Fiber also aids in weight control by keeping you fuller for longer periods.

Adding greens to your smoothies helps to regulate blood sugar levels, and the high fiber content of greens helps slow carbohydrate digestion. Smoothies are also more filling than juices, leaving you satiated and less likely to overeat during the day. Replacing a meal with a smoothie is an easy way to cut down calories and promote weight loss.

Furthermore, blending is more cost-effective than juicing since it requires fewer fruits and vegetables to make a smoothie of the same size as a glass of juice. Smoothies also keep you fuller for longer, which means you don't have to purchase additional food during the day. Blending is also less time-consuming since you can throw all the fruits and vegetables into the blender at once, while juicing requires cutting everything up small enough to fit into the juicer.

Cleaning up after blending is also easier and faster since blenders do not have any disassemblable parts that require thorough cleaning. Juicers, on the other hand, must be taken apart and cleaned after every use, which takes up a lot of time and can be tedious. Additionally, adding superfoods like maca or acai berries to smoothies is more straightforward since they blend evenly through the mixture, while juicing requires extra steps to incorporate superfoods.

In conclusion, blending offers more health benefits than juicing due to its higher fiber content, satiety-inducing properties, cost-effectiveness, and faster preparation and cleanup times. With the variety of ingredients available, smoothies can be customized to suit individual preferences and dietary needs, making them a delicious and healthy addition to your daily routine.

HOW TO CHOOSE A BLENDER FOR MAKING GREEN SMOOTHIES

Making green smoothies is a great way to incorporate healthy fruits and vegetables into your diet, but choosing the right blender can be overwhelming. With so many options available on the market, it can be hard to know where to start. Here are some key factors to consider when choosing a blender for making green smoothies.

Power: A high-powered blender is essential for making smooth and creamy green smoothies. Look for a blender with a wattage of at least 500, although a more powerful motor will be better. This will ensure that the blender can handle tough ingredients like kale and frozen fruits without leaving behind any lumps or chunks.

Size: Blenders come in a variety of sizes, so consider how much smoothie you want to make at once. If you're just making smoothies for yourself, a small personal blender may be sufficient. However, if you plan to make smoothies for your whole family, a larger blender with a 64-ounce pitcher might be a better option.

Blade Quality: The blades in the blender are responsible for chopping up the ingredients, so it's important to choose a blender with high-quality blades. Stainless steel blades are the best because they are strong and durable, and they will not rust over time.

Ease of Use and Cleaning: Making smoothies should be easy, so look for a blender that is user-friendly and easy to clean. Some blenders have multiple settings for different types of blending, while others may only have an on/off switch. Look for a blender with a removable blade that is easy to clean.

Price: Blenders come in a range of prices, from under $50 to over $500. Consider how often you will be using the blender and what features are important to you. While it's important to invest in a quality blender, there are affordable options available that will still deliver great results.

In conclusion, choosing the right blender for making green smoothies requires careful consideration of several key factors, including power, size, blade quality, ease of use and cleaning, and price. By keeping these factors in mind, you can choose a blender that will make delicious and healthy smoothies for years to come.

Bonus Tips

Breakfast Sweet Smoothies
A nutritious breakfast smoothie gives a good start to your day. It gives you the energy to keep going all day long. In the summer, people around the world look for ways to blend flavor and good nutrition together and get relief from the scorching heat. Having smoothies with breakfast every day can surely pave the way for good health and enjoyment throughout the hot season.

It also prevents dehydration: Water is the most abundant thing both on earth and in your body. About 70 percent of your body is water. Having breakfast smoothies is a great way to replenish the loss of water in your body during the summer.

Detoxifies your body
Foods like garlic, papaya, and beets help cleanse your blood and get rid of several toxins accumulated in your body tissues. Thus, to have a great breakfast you should include smoothies as reliable detoxifying drinks every day.

Keeps Blood Sugar in Check
High blood sugar and diabetes are the most common lifestyle diseases that bother people all around the world. People who have imbalanced sugar levels in their blood are prone to several complications. Thus having a breakfast that is rich in nutrients but low in calories can make things easier.

Lunch Smoothies

Makes you feel full: People trying to lose weight often skip the morning meal and end up snacking on food in larger amounts between meals. To avoid this, experts advise having smoothies made of excellent fruits and flavors so that you stay full for a long time.

Controls Cravings
Smoothies are full of nutrients and flavor. They are an essential part of the best luches, as they provide a power-packed start for the day. A lot of protein along with many nutrients subdue food cravings and keep you away from eating junk food.

Boosts Brain Power
It is quite evident that certain fruits and vegetables increase brain power and boost memory. Mental alertness and concentration is greatly enhanced by ingredients like coconut that are rich in omega-3 fatty acids. Smoothies with these ingredients help the brain work faster.

Dinner Green Smoothies
Health and nutrition experts worldwide suggest consuming liquid food for better digestion. Smoothies contain blended fruits and vegetables in liquid form that make it easier for the body to break them down.

Curbs Better Digestion
People belonging to different age groups around the world often face issues related to lack of sleep and restlessness. A healthy dinner accompanied by a smoothie made of bananas, kiwi, and oats provides calcium and magnesium in good amounts. This induces sleep and helps maintain healthy sleeping patterns.

Aid in Digestion
Green smoothies that contain a lot of green leafy vegetables add essential vitamins and minerals to dinner and aid in digestion. The fiber supplied by these drinks multiplies the benefits of having a delicious dinner smoothie, especially during the summer.

Provides a Good Amount of Fiber
The most common problem people suffer from today is related to upset bowels. A good amount of fibrous food is essential for regulating the excretory system so that you can enjoy summer without worrying about your health. Smoothies with a lot of fruits and vegetables help keep your bowels functioning smoothly.

RECIPES

RASPBERRY BANANA GREEN SMOOTHIE

This green smoothie is a great source of vitamins and minerals, especially vitamin C and potassium from the raspberries and banana, and vitamin K and folate from the spinach. It's also low in calories and fat, and high in fiber, making it a great option for a healthy snack or breakfast.

Calories: 94
Fat: 2 g
Carb: 22 g
Protein: 2 g
Fiber: 6 g
Time: 5 min
Servings: 2

- 2 cups fresh spinach
- 1 ripe banana
- 1 cup fresh raspberries
- 1 cup unsweetened almond milk
- 1 tbsp honey (optional)

Ingredients

Instructions

1. Rinse the spinach and raspberries.
2. Peel the banana and break it into chunks.
3. Combine all the ingredients in a blender and blend until smooth.
4. Taste and add honey if desired for sweetness.

STRAWBERRY BANANA GREEN SMOOTHIE

This green smoothie is a great source of vitamins and minerals, especially vitamin C and potassium from the strawberries and banana, and vitamin K and folate from the spinach. The chia seeds provide protein, healthy fats, and additional fiber, making this smoothie a filling and nutritious breakfast or snack option. It's also low in calories, making it a great choice for those looking to manage their weight.

Calories: 159
Fat: 6 g
Carb: 28 g
Protein: 2 g
Fiber: 10 g
Time: 5 min
Servings: 2

- 2 cups fresh spinach
- 1 ripe banana
- 1 cup fresh strawberries
- 1 cup unsweetened almond milk
- 1 tbsp chia seeds
- 1 tbsp honey (optional)

Ingredients

Instructions

1. Rinse the spinach and strawberries.
2. Peel the banana and break it into chunks.
3. Combine all the ingredients in a blender and blend until smooth.
4. Taste and add honey if desired for sweetness.

CELERY APPLE AND KIWI SMOOTHIE

This green smoothie is a great source of vitamin C, fiber, and antioxidants from the apples and kiwis. The celery provides additional fiber and a refreshing crunch. This smoothie is low in calories and fat, making it a great choice for those watching their weight or looking for a light and refreshing snack.

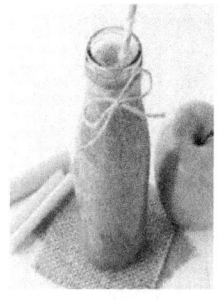

Calories: 87
Fat: 0 g
Carb: 22 g
Protein: 1 g
Fiber: 5 g
Time: 5 min
Servings: 2

Ingredients
- 2 cups chopped celery
- 1 medium apple, cored and chopped
- 2 kiwis, peeled and chopped
- 1 cup water
- 1 cup ice

Instructions

1. Wash and chop the celery, apple, and kiwis.
2. Add the chopped ingredients to a blender along with the water and ice.
3. Blend until smooth.
4. Taste and adjust sweetness, if necessary, by adding a small amount of honey or maple syrup.

PINEAPPLE MINT SMOOTHIE WITH PISTACHIOS

This green smoothie is a great source of vitamins and minerals, especially vitamin C and potassium from the pineapple, and iron and calcium from the spinach. The pistachios provide protein, healthy fats, and additional fiber, making this smoothie a filling and nutritious breakfast or snack option. The mint leaves give a refreshing taste and help with digestion. It's also low in sugar and high in fiber, making it a great choice for those looking to manage their weight or blood sugar levels.

Calories: 219
Fat: 11 g
Carb: 26 g
Protein: 7 g
Fiber: 5 g
Time: 5 min
Servings: 2
Ingredients

- 2 cups fresh spinach
- 2 cups diced pineapple
- 1/4 cup shelled pistachios
- 1/4 cup fresh mint leaves
- 1 cup unsweetened almond milk
- 1 tbsp honey (optional)

Instructions

1. Rinse the spinach and mint leaves.
2. Combine all the ingredients in a blender and blend until smooth.
3. Taste and add honey if desired for sweetness.

CHERRY VANILLA GREEN SMOOTHIE

This green smoothie is a great source of vitamins and minerals, especially vitamin C and antioxidants from the cherries, and calcium and protein from the Greek yogurt. The spinach provides additional fiber, iron, and potassium. The vanilla extract adds a sweet flavor without adding sugar. It's also low in calories and fat, making it a great choice for those watching their weight or looking for a light and refreshing snack.

Calories: 123
Fat: 2 g
Carb: 18 g
Protein: 10 g
Fiber: 4 g
Time: 5 min
Servings: 2

Ingredients
- 2 cups fresh spinach
- 1 cup frozen cherries
- 1/2 cup plain Greek yogurt
- 1/2 cup unsweetened almond milk
- 1 tsp vanilla extract
- 1 tbsp honey (optional)

Instructions

1. Rinse the spinach and remove any tough stems.
2. Combine all the ingredients in a blender and blend until smooth.
3. Taste and add honey if desired for sweetness.

MANGO BANANA GREEN SMOOTHIE

This green smoothie is a great source of vitamins and minerals, especially vitamin C, vitamin A, and potassium from the mango and banana, and iron, calcium, and folate from the spinach. The chia seeds add additional fiber, healthy fats, and protein, making this smoothie a filling and nutritious breakfast or snack option. The turmeric adds anti-inflammatory properties, while the coconut milk gives it a rich and creamy texture. It's also naturally sweet and low in sugar, making it a great choice for those looking to manage their blood sugar levels.

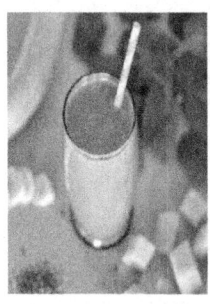

Calories: 219
Fat: 8 g
Carb: 37 g
Protein: 6 g
Fiber: 4 g
Time: 5 min
Servings: 2
Ingredients

- 2 cups fresh spinach
- 1 ripe mango, peeled and diced
- 1 ripe banana, peeled and sliced
- 1 cup unsweetened coconut milk
- 1/2 tsp ground turmeric
- 1 tbsp chia seeds

Instructions

1. Rinse the spinach and remove any tough stems.
2. Combine all the ingredients in a blender and blend until smooth.
3. Taste and adjust the sweetness by adding a little bit of honey or maple syrup if desired.

PINEAPPLE COCONUT GREEN SMOOTHIE

This green smoothie is a great source of vitamins and minerals, especially vitamin C, vitamin K, and potassium from the pineapple and kale, and calcium, iron, and folate from the kale. The chia seeds add additional fiber, healthy fats, and protein, making this smoothie a filling and nutritious breakfast or snack option. The shredded coconut adds a tropical flavor and a little bit of healthy fat. The coconut milk makes this smoothie creamy and delicious without adding any sugar. It's a perfect way to get a boost of nutrients and energy to start your day.

Calories: 223
Fat: 11 g
Carb: 31 g
Protein: 7 g
Fiber: 9 g
Time: 5 min
Servings: 2

Ingredients

- 2 cups chopped kale leaves, tough stems removed
- 1 cup chopped fresh pineapple
- 1 ripe banana, peeled and sliced
- 1 cup unsweetened coconut milk
- 1/4 cup unsweetened shredded coconut
- 1 tbsp chia seeds

Instructions

1. Rinse the kale leaves and remove any tough stems.
2. Combine all the ingredients in a blender and blend until smooth.
3. Taste and adjust the sweetness by adding a little bit of honey or maple syrup if desired.

PEACH MANGO GREEN SMOOTHIE

This green smoothie is a great source of vitamins and minerals, especially vitamin C, vitamin A, and potassium from the mango and peaches, and calcium and protein from the Greek yogurt. The spinach provides additional fiber, iron, and folate. The almond milk adds a creamy texture and a little bit of healthy fat. The banana adds natural sweetness and creaminess to the smoothie. It's a perfect way to start your day or as a healthy snack during the day.

Calories: 191
Fat: 3 g
Carb: 38 g
Protein: 8 g
Fiber: 6 g
Time: 5 min
Servings: 2

Ingredients
- 2 cups fresh spinach
- 1 cup chopped fresh mango
- 1 cup chopped fresh peaches
- 1 ripe banana, peeled and sliced
- 1/2 cup plain Greek yogurt
- 1/2 cup unsweetened almond milk

Instructions

1. Rinse the spinach and remove any tough stems.
2. Combine all the ingredients in a blender and blend until smooth.
3. Taste and adjust the sweetness by adding a little bit of honey or maple syrup if desired.

RASPBERRY PINEAPPLE GREEN SMOOTHIE

This green smoothie is a great source of vitamins and minerals, especially vitamin C, vitamin A, and potassium from the pineapple and raspberries, and calcium and vitamin E from the almond milk. The kale provides additional fiber, iron, and folate. The maple syrup adds natural sweetness to the smoothie. It's a refreshing and nutritious drink that can be enjoyed as a healthy breakfast or snack.

Calories: 112
Fat: 3 g
Carb: 21 g
Protein: 3 g
Fiber: 7 g
Time: 5 min
Servings: 2

Ingredients
- 2 cups kale, washed and chopped
- 1 cup chopped pineapple
- 1 cup raspberries
- 1 cup unsweetened almond milk
- 1 tbsp maple syrup

Instructions
1. Rinse the kale and remove any tough stems.
2. Combine all the ingredients in a blender and blend until smooth.
3. Taste and adjust the sweetness by adding more maple syrup if desired.

ORANGE CARROT GREEN SMOOTHIE

This green smoothie is a great source of vitamin C from the oranges, vitamin A from the carrots, and iron and calcium from the spinach. The coconut water provides hydration and natural sweetness without added sugar, and the honey adds additional sweetness and antioxidants. It's a refreshing and nutritious drink that can be enjoyed as a healthy breakfast or snack.

Calories: 112
Fat: 3 g
Carb: 21 g
Protein: 3 g
Fiber: 7 g
Time: 5 min
Servings: 2

Ingredients
- 2 oranges, peeled and chopped
- 2 carrots, peeled and chopped
- 2 cups spinach
- 1 cup coconut water
- 1 tbsp honey

Instructions

1. Rinse the spinach leaves and remove any tough stems.
2. Combine all the ingredients in a blender and blend until smooth.
3. Taste and adjust the sweetness by adding more honey if desired.

APPLE BERRY GREEN SMOOTHIE

This green smoothie is rich in antioxidants, vitamins, and minerals. The blueberries provide a dose of vitamin C and fiber, while the apple adds natural sweetness and more fiber. The spinach and spring mix greens offer a boost of iron, calcium, and folate. The ground flaxseeds provide omega-3 fatty acids and fiber, which can help promote digestive health. This smoothie can be enjoyed as a quick and nutritious breakfast or snack.

Calories: 254
Fat: 6 g
Carb: 53 g
Protein: 5 g
Fiber: 16 g
Time: 5 min
Servings: 2

- 1 apple, cored and quartered
- 1 banana, peeled
- 2 cups frozen blueberries
- 2 handfuls of spinach
- 1 handful of spring mix greens
- 2 cups water
- 1 packet stevia (optional)
- 2 tablespoons ground flaxseeds

Ingredients

Instructions

1. Wash the spinach and spring mix greens.
2. Blend all ingredients in a blender until smooth and creamy.
3. If needed, adjust the sweetness by adding stevia.

BERRY PEACHY GREEN SMOOTHIE

This Berry Peachy green smoothie is a nutritious and delicious way to start your day. The kale and spinach are packed with vitamins and minerals, while the frozen peaches and mixed berries provide a good source of fiber and antioxidants. The ground flaxseeds are a good source of omega-3 fatty acids and fiber. This smoothie is not only tasty but also filling and satisfying. It can be enjoyed as a breakfast or a snack.

Calories: 235
Fat: 4 g
Carb: 53 g
Protein: 5 g
Fiber: 16 g
Time: 5 min
Servings: 2

Ingredients
- 2 handfuls of kale
- 1 handful of spinach
- 2 cups water
- 2 apples, cored and quartered
- 2 cups frozen peaches
- 2 cups frozen mixed berries
- 2 packets stevia (optional)
- 2 tablespoons ground flaxseeds

Instructions

1. Wash the kale and spinach.
2. Add all the ingredients to a blender and blend until smooth and creamy.
3. If needed, adjust the sweetness by adding stevia.

SPINACH KALE BERRY SMOOTHIE

This green smoothie is a powerhouse of nutrition, thanks to the combination of kale, spinach, berries, and flaxseeds. Kale and spinach are both rich in vitamins A, C, and K, while berries are a great source of antioxidants and fiber. Flaxseeds are a good source of omega-3 fatty acids and fiber. The apple and banana add natural sweetness to the smoothie, and stevia provides additional sweetness without adding calories. Enjoy this delicious and nutritious smoothie as a healthy breakfast or snack.

Calories: 200
Fat: 4 g
Carb: 42 g
Protein: 4 g
Fiber: 12 g
Time: 5 min
Servings: 2

- 1 handful kale
- 1 handful spinach
- 1 cup water
- 1 apple, cored and quartered
- 1 banana, peeled
- 2 cups frozen blueberries
- 2 packets stevia
- 2 tablespoons ground flaxseeds

Ingredients

Instructions

1. In a blender, combine the kale, spinach, and water. Blend until smooth.
2. Add the apple, banana, frozen blueberries, stevia, and ground flaxseeds. Blend until smooth and creamy.
3. Pour the smoothie into two glasses and enjoy!

PEACH BANANA GREEN SMOOTHIE

This green smoothie is packed with nutrients and antioxidants from the spinach and peaches. The banana provides natural sweetness and potassium, while the sunflower oil adds healthy fats. Spirulina is a nutrient-dense superfood that is high in protein, iron, and antioxidants. This smoothie is a great way to start your day or refuel after a workout.

Calories: 244
Fat: 8 g
Carb: 43 g
Protein: 4 g
Fiber: 6 g
Time: 5 min
Servings: 2

Ingredients
- 2 cups spinach
- 1 cup water
- 2 cups frozen peaches
- 1 banana, peeled
- 1 tablespoon sunflower oil
- 2 teaspoons spirulina

Instructions

1. Add spinach and water to a blender and blend until smooth.
2. Add frozen peaches, banana, sunflower oil, and spirulina to the blender and blend until smooth.
3. Pour the smoothie into glasses and serve.

WATERMELON GINGER GREEN SMOOTHIE

This Watermelon Ginger Greens smoothie is packed with refreshing flavors and healthy nutrients. The watermelon is a great source of vitamins A and C, while the ginger provides anti-inflammatory and immune-boosting benefits. The lettuce adds additional vitamins and minerals, and the chia seeds provide a boost of fiber and healthy omega-3 fatty acids. Enjoy this smoothie as a refreshing and nutritious drink any time of day!

Calories: 115
Fat: 4 g
Carb: 20 g
Protein: 3 g
Fiber: 8 g
Time: 5 min
Servings: 2

Ingredients
- 2 cups lettuce
- 1 cup ice
- 2 cups watermelon chunks
- 2 tablespoons chia seeds
- 1 inch fresh ginger, peeled
- 1/2 cup water

Instructions

1. Blend the lettuce and water together until smooth.
2. Add the watermelon chunks and ginger to the blender and blend until smooth.
3. Add in the chia seeds and blend briefly to combine.
4. Serve the smoothie immediately.

BANANA CHIA GREEN SMOOTHIE

This smoothie is packed with potassium from the bananas, which can help regulate blood pressure and support heart health. The almond milk provides healthy fats, while the chia seeds add protein and fiber for sustained energy. The lettuce adds additional vitamins and minerals, making this a nutritious and filling breakfast or snack option.

Calories: 277
Fat: 8 g
Carb: 52 g
Protein: 7 g
Fiber: 14 g
Time: 5 min
Servings: 2

Ingredients
- 2 cups lettuce
- 2 cups almond milk
- 2 bananas, peeled
- 2 tablespoons chia seeds

Instructions

1. Wash and dry the lettuce, and tear it into smaller pieces.
2. Add the lettuce, almond milk, bananas, and chia seeds to a blender.
3. Blend until smooth and creamy.
4. Pour into glasses and serve immediately.

CHERRY WHEATGRASS GREEN SMOOTHIE

This Cherry Wheatgrass Green Smoothie is loaded with vitamins, minerals, and antioxidants. Spinach is a great source of iron and vitamin K, while cherries are packed with vitamin C and antioxidants. Wheatgrass is known for its high nutritional value and detoxifying properties, and beet juice is a great source of potassium and other essential nutrients. Chia seeds and dates add fiber and natural sweetness to the smoothie, making it a delicious and healthy drink that can be enjoyed at any time of the day.

Calories: 217
Fat: 5 g
Carb: 44 g
Protein: 6 g
Fiber: 13 g
Time: 5 min
Servings: 2

Ingredients
- Handful of spinach
- 1 cup water
- 1 cup frozen cherries
- 1 cup fresh wheatgrass juice
- 1 cup fresh beet juice
- 1/4 cup chia seeds
- 2 large pitted dates

Instructions

1. Blend the spinach and water until smooth.
2. Add the frozen cherries and blend again.
3. Pour in the wheatgrass juice and beet juice and blend until well combined.
4. Add the chia seeds and pitted dates and blend until the smoothie is thick and creamy.
5. Pour into glasses and enjoy!

BERRY PROTEIN GREEN SMOOTHIE

This Berry Protein Greens smoothie is a delicious and nutrient-packed drink that can be enjoyed as a healthy breakfast or post-workout snack. The combination of frozen raspberries and blueberries provides a good source of vitamin C and antioxidants, while the almond butter and plant-based protein powder add protein and healthy fats. Cacao powder is a great source of magnesium and iron, and the lettuce adds extra vitamins and fiber to the mix.

Calories: 370
Fat: 17 g
Carb: 33 g
Protein: 23 g
Fiber: 16 g
Time: 5 min
Servings: 2

Ingredients
- 2 handfuls of lettuce
- 2 cups of water
- 2 cups of frozen raspberries
- 1/4 cup of frozen blueberries
- 1/4 cup of almond butter
- 1/4 cup of cacao powder
- 1/2 cup of plant-based protein powder

Instructions

1. Blend lettuce and water until smooth.
2. Add frozen raspberries and blueberries and blend until smooth.
3. Add almond butter, cacao powder, and plant-based protein powder, and blend until smooth.
4. Serve chilled.

BERRY SEEDS SPINACH GREEN SMOOTHIE

This green smoothie is a delicious and nutritious way to start your day! The spinach provides a great source of iron and other important vitamins and minerals, while the blueberries and dried fruit add natural sweetness and antioxidants. The sunflower seeds and chia seeds are a good source of healthy fats, fiber, and protein, making this smoothie a well-rounded and filling meal.

Calories: 411
Fat: 23 g
Carb: 33 g
Protein: 49 g
Fiber: 22 g
Time: 5 min
Servings: 2

Ingredients
- 2 cups spinach
- 2 cups water
- 1 cup frozen blueberries
- 1/2 cup sunflower seeds
- 1/2 cup chia seeds
- 6 dried figs
- 3 pitted dates
- 1/4 cup cacao powder

Instructions

1. Blend spinach and water until smooth.
2. Add frozen blueberries, sunflower seeds, chia seeds, dried figs, pitted dates, and cacao powder to the blender.
3. Blend until smooth and creamy.
4. Pour into glasses and enjoy!

NUT CELERY PROTEIN GREEN SMOOTHIE

This green smoothie is a delicious and nutritious way to start your day or refuel after a workout. It's packed with protein from the macadamia nuts and plant-based protein powder, and the celery adds a refreshing crunch. The dates provide natural sweetness and a boost of energy, while the wheatgrass juice is rich in vitamins and minerals. Enjoy!

Calories: 440
Fat: 32 g
Carb: 35 g
Protein: 30 g
Fiber: 10 g
Time: 5 min
Servings: 2

Ingredients
- 1 handful of greens (such as spinach or kale)
- 2 cups of water
- 1 cup of macadamia nuts
- 1/4 cup of fresh wheatgrass juice
- 2 large pitted dates
- 1/2 cup of chopped celery
- 1/2 cup of plant-based protein powder

Instructions

1. Add the greens and water to a blender and blend until smooth.
2. Add the macadamia nuts, wheatgrass juice, dates, and celery to the blender and blend again until smooth.
3. Finally, add the protein powder and blend until well combined.
4. Serve the smoothie immediately or store it in the refrigerator for later.

MANGO MATCHA GREEN SMOOTHIE

This green smoothie is a delicious and healthy way to start your day. It's loaded with nutrient-dense ingredients like spinach, mango, and avocado, and also contains matcha powder for an extra boost of antioxidants and caffeine. The chia seeds add a crunchy texture and are a great source of fiber, while the honey provides a touch of sweetness. Overall, this smoothie is a tasty and satisfying breakfast or snack option that will leave you feeling energized and refreshed.

Calories: 440
Fat: 32 g
Carb: 35 g
Protein: 30 g
Fiber: 10 g
Time: 5 min
Servings: 2

Ingredients
- 2 cups baby spinach
- 1 cup water
- 2 ripe mangoes, peeled and chopped
- 1 tsp matcha powder
- 1/2 avocado, peeled and pitted
- 1 tbsp honey
- 1 tbsp chia seeds

Instructions

1. Add the baby spinach and water to a blender and blend until smooth.
2. Add the chopped mango, matcha powder, avocado, and honey to the blender and blend until smooth.
3. If the smoothie is too thick, add more water as needed.
4. Pour the smoothie into glasses and sprinkle chia seeds on top.
5. Serve and enjoy!

GREEN SPIRULINA SMOOTHIE

This Green Spirulina Smoothie is packed with nutrients and is a great way to start your day. The spinach provides a great source of vitamins and minerals, while the banana and avocado add creaminess and sweetness. Spirulina is a superfood that is high in protein and antioxidants, making it a great addition to this smoothie. The chia seeds provide a boost of fiber and omega-3 fatty acids, and the almond milk adds a touch of creaminess without any added sugars. Enjoy this smoothie as a nutritious breakfast or snack.

Calories: 210
Fat: 12 g
Carb: 27 g
Protein: 6 g
Fiber: 9 g
Time: 5 min
Servings: 2

Ingredients

- 2 cups spinach
- 1 banana, peeled
- 1/2 avocado, pitted and peeled
- 1 tsp spirulina powder
- 1/2 cup unsweetened almond milk
- 1 tbsp chia seeds
- 1 tbsp honey (optional)

Instructions

1. Add the spinach, banana, avocado, spirulina powder, almond milk, chia seeds, and honey (if using) to a blender.
2. Blend until smooth and creamy.
3. Divide the smoothie between two glasses and serve immediately.

COLD BUSTER CITRUS GREEN SMOOTHIE

This refreshing green smoothie is packed with vitamin C from the oranges, protein from the Greek yogurt and optional protein powder, and fiber from the baby spinach. The addition of ginger provides anti-inflammatory benefits, while turmeric powder adds a warm, earthy flavor and potential anti-inflammatory properties. The optional honey adds natural sweetness, while the lemon juice and zest add a citrusy brightness. Enjoy this smoothie as a healthy breakfast or post-workout snack.

Calories: 135
Fat: 2 g
Carb: 28 g
Protein: 8 g
Fiber: 5 g
Time: 5 min
Servings: 2

Ingredients
- 1 (5.3 – 6 oz.) container blood orange Greek yogurt
- 1 tbsp. lemon juice + ½ tsp. lemon zest
- 2 oranges, peeled
- ¼ tsp. turmeric powder
- 1 tsp. grated ginger
- 2 cups packed baby spinach
- ½ cup ice
- honey (optional)
- protein powder (optional)

Instructions

1. Add the blood orange Greek yogurt, lemon juice, lemon zest, peeled oranges, turmeric powder, grated ginger, and packed baby spinach to a blender.
2. Blend the ingredients on high speed until smooth.
3. Add ice to the blender and continue blending until the mixture is thick and creamy.
4. If desired, add honey to sweeten the smoothie to your liking.
5. For an extra protein boost, add a scoop of protein powder to the blender and blend until smooth.
6. Pour the smoothie into two glasses and enjoy immediately.

BERRY PUMPKIN PROTEIN GREEN SMOOTHIE

This green smoothie is a great source of protein, fiber, and essential nutrients. The lettuce and celery provide fiber and antioxidants, while the pumpkin seeds and goji berries add healthy fats and vitamins. The plant-based protein powder and maca powder give a protein boost and energy to start your day. Enjoy this delicious and nutritious smoothie as a healthy breakfast or snack option.

Calories: 284
Fat: 10 g
Carb: 32 g
Protein: 18 g
Fiber: 10 g
Time: 5 min
Servings: 2

Ingredients

- 1 cup lettuce
- 1 cup chopped celery
- 2 cups water
- 1/4 cup pumpkin seeds
- 1/4 cup goji berries
- 2 pitted dates
- 1/4 cup plant-based protein powder
- 2 tablespoons maca powder

Instructions

1. Rinse the lettuce and chop it into small pieces.
2. Rinse and chop the celery into small pieces.
3. In a blender, add the lettuce, celery, water, pumpkin seeds, goji berries, pitted dates, plant-based protein powder, and maca powder. Blend on high speed until smooth and creamy. Serve immediately and enjoy!

PAPAYA LEMON GREEN SMOOTHIE

This green smoothie is a refreshing and nutritious drink that combines the cleansing power of parsley with the tropical sweetness of papaya and banana. The lemon juice adds a bright and zesty flavor while also providing a boost of vitamin C. It's a great way to start your day or as a mid-day snack to keep you feeling energized and healthy.

Calories: 140
Fat: 1 g
Carb: 36 g
Protein: 2 g
Fiber: 5 g
Time: 5 min
Servings: 2

Ingredients
- 1 handful parsley
- 2 cups water
- 1 banana, peeled and frozen
- 1 cup papaya chunks
- 1/2 lemon, juiced

Instructions

1. Wash the parsley and add it to a blender with the water.
2. Blend until smooth.
3. Add the frozen banana, papaya chunks, and lemon juice to the blender.
4. Blend again until smooth and creamy.
5. Taste and adjust sweetness with honey, if desired.
6. Pour into glasses and enjoy immediately.

MULTIFRUIT GREEN SMOOTHIE

This green smoothie is a delicious and nutritious way to start your day or refuel after a workout. It's packed with protein from the Greek yogurt and whey protein powder, as well as a variety of fruits and vegetables that provide vitamins, minerals, and fiber. The kale adds an extra boost of nutrients, while the pineapple and green grapes provide natural sweetness without any added sugars. Enjoy this smoothie as a healthy meal or snack anytime!

Calories: 230
Fat: 1 g
Carb: 32 g
Protein: 25 g
Fiber: 5 g
Time: 5 min
Servings: 2

Ingredients
- 3/4 cup plain Greek yogurt
- 1 scoop whey isolate protein powder
- 1/2 cup green grapes
- 1 kiwi, peeled
- 1 banana, peeled
- 1 green apple, cored
- 1/2 cup pineapple
- 1/2 cup kale, stems removed
- 6 ice cubes

Instructions

1. Add all ingredients to a blender.
2. Blend until smooth and creamy.
3. Adjust consistency with water, if necessary.

CUCUMBER STRAWBERRY GREEN SMOOTHIE

This green smoothie is a great source of vitamins and minerals from the greens, cucumber, strawberries, and dried figs. The ground flaxseeds add healthy fats and fiber to keep you full and satisfied. It's a delicious and nutritious way to start your day or refuel after a workout.

Calories: 135
Fat: 4 g
Carb: 25 g
Protein: 4 g
Fiber: 8 g
Time: 5 min
Servings: 2

Ingredients
- 2 handfuls of greens (spinach, kale, or chard)
- 1 cup of water
- 1/2 cucumber, chopped
- 1 cup frozen strawberries
- 3 dried figs, chopped
- 2 tablespoons ground flaxseeds

Instructions

1. Add the water and greens to a blender and blend until smooth.
2. Add the cucumber, frozen strawberries, dried figs, and ground flaxseeds to the blender and blend until smooth.
3. If the smoothie is too thick, add more water until it reaches your desired consistency.
4. Pour the smoothie into two glasses and enjoy!

BANANA NUT GREEN SMOOTHIE

This green smoothie is packed with fiber and nutrients from the lettuce, bananas, cacao powder, and ground flaxseeds. The almond milk adds a creamy texture and a source of healthy fats, making it a filling and satisfying breakfast or snack. The cacao powder provides a rich chocolate flavor and antioxidants, while the ground flaxseeds add additional fiber and omega-3 fatty acids. It's a delicious and healthy way to start your day!

Calories: 252
Fat: 7 g
Carb: 46 g
Protein: 7 g
Fiber: 11 g
Time: 5 min
Servings: 2

- 2 cups of lettuce
- 1 cup of unsweetened almond milk
- 2 ripe bananas, peeled and frozen
- 2 tablespoons of cacao powder
- 2 tablespoons of ground flaxseeds

Ingredients

Instructions

1. Wash the lettuce leaves thoroughly and chop them into small pieces.
2. Add the chopped lettuce to a blender along with the almond milk.
3. Blend until the mixture is smooth.
4. Add the frozen bananas, cacao powder, and ground flaxseeds to the blender.
5. Blend everything together until the mixture is creamy and smooth.
6. Pour the smoothie into two glasses and serve immediately.

VANILLA-MINT GREEN SMOOTHIE

This Vanilla-Mint Green Smoothie is a delicious and refreshing way to start your day or to enjoy as a healthy snack. Packed with fresh spinach and mint leaves, it provides a great source of vitamins and minerals. The coconut milk adds a creamy texture and healthy fats to keep you feeling full and satisfied. Enjoy the delicious vanilla and mint flavors for a tasty treat that is also good for you!

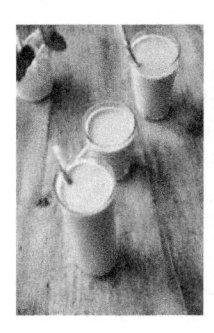

Calories: 114
Fat: 5 g
Carb: 19 g
Protein: 3 g
Fiber: 3 g
Time: 5 min
Servings: 2

Ingredients
- 1/2 frozen banana
- 1 1/2 cups fresh spinach
- 10-15 fresh mint leaves
- 1/4 cup coconut milk

Instructions
1. Add all ingredients to a blender.
2. Blend until smooth and creamy.
3. If the smoothie is too thick, add a splash of water or more coconut milk until desired consistency is reached.
4. Pour into glasses and enjoy!

TROPICAL GREEN SMOOTHIE

This green smoothie is a great source of vitamins A and C from the spinach and pineapple, and also provides potassium and fiber from the banana and mango. The milk adds protein and calcium, while the optional berries add extra antioxidants and flavor. Sweetener can be added to taste, and options such as honey, agave nectar, or maple syrup can be used. This smoothie makes for a healthy and tasty breakfast or snack option.

Calories: 282
Fat: 2 g
Carb: 68 g
Protein: 6 g
Fiber: 38 g
Time: 5 min
Servings: 2

- 1/2 frozen banana
- 1 to 2 cups frozen spinach
- 1 cup frozen pineapple chunks
- 1 cup frozen mango chunks
- 1 medium ripe banana, peeled
- 1 cup milk
- 1 tsp. vanilla extract
- Sweetener, to taste
- Optional: 1 cup strawberries, blueberries, raspberries, or a favorite berry

Ingredients
Instructions

1. Add the frozen banana, frozen spinach, frozen pineapple chunks, frozen mango chunks, and milk to a blender.
2. Blend until smooth.
3. Add the ripe banana, vanilla extract, sweetener, and optional berries to the blender.
4. Blend until smooth and creamy.
5. Pour into glasses and serve immediately.

BASIL CANTALOUPE GREEN SMOOTHIE

This green smoothie is a great source of vitamins A and C from the spinach and cantaloupe, and also provides fiber and antioxidants from the pear and basil. Camu camu powder adds additional vitamin C, while pea protein provides plant-based protein. This smoothie is low in calories and fat, making it a great option for a light breakfast or snack.

Calories: 85
Fat: 1 g
Carb: 18 g
Protein: 4 g
Fiber: 4 g
Time: 5 min
Servings: 2

Ingredients

- 1 1/2 oz. baby spinach
- 4 oz. cantaloupe
- 1 pear, chopped
- 4 leaves basil
- 1 tsp. camu camu powder
- 1 tbsp. pea protein
- 1 cup water
- 1 cup ice

Instructions

1. Add the baby spinach, cantaloupe, pear, basil, camu camu powder, and pea protein to a blender.
2. Add water and ice to the blender.
3. Blend until smooth and creamy.
4. Pour into glasses and serve immediately.

BANANA BLUEBERRY GOOSEBERRY GREEN SMOOTHIE

This green smoothie is a great source of fiber from the fruits and flaxseed, and also provides vitamins and minerals such as vitamin C and potassium from the blueberries and banana. Almond butter provides healthy fats and protein, while raw agave adds sweetness without the use of refined sugar. This smoothie is a healthy and delicious way to start your day or as a post-workout recovery drink.

Calories: 224
Fat: 10 g
Carb: 32 g
Protein: 5 g
Fiber: 7 g
Time: 5 min
Servings: 2

Ingredients

- 1 1/2 cups almond milk
- 1 big handful spinach
- 1 cup fresh blueberries
- 1/2 cup sliced banana (approximately 1 banana)
- 1/2 cup cape gooseberries
- 1 tbsp. flaxseed
- 1 tbsp. almond butter
- 1 tbsp. raw agave

Instructions

1. Add the almond milk, spinach, blueberries, sliced banana, cape gooseberries, flaxseed, almond butter, and raw agave to a blender.
2. Blend until smooth and creamy.
3. Pour into glasses and serve immediately.

ORANGE AVOCADO GREEN SMOOTHIE

The spirulina powder is a great source of plant-based protein, while the avocado provides healthy fats and creaminess to the smoothie. The oranges add a sweet and tangy flavor while also providing vitamin C. This smoothie is perfect for a healthy breakfast or snack.

Calories: 380
Fat: 17 g
Carb: 32 g
Protein: 47 g
Fiber: 12 g
Time: 5 min
Servings: 2

Ingredients

- 2 handfuls of mixed greens (spinach, kale, or chard)
- 1 cup of water
- 1 cup of ice
- 2 oranges, peeled
- 1 avocado, peeled and pitted
- 2 teaspoons of spirulina powder

Instructions

1. Wash and prepare the greens by removing any tough stems or parts.
2. Add the greens, water, and ice to a blender.
3. Blend on high until the ice is crushed and the greens are well blended.
4. Add the peeled oranges, peeled and pitted avocado, and spirulina powder to the blender.

COCONUT OIL DETOX GREEN SMOOTHIE

This smoothie is a great way to get in your daily dose of greens and healthy fats, and the addition of spirulina powder provides a boost of plant-based protein and antioxidants. It's perfect as a breakfast or post-workout snack.

Calories: 360
Fat: 32 g
Carb: 22 g
Protein: 47 g
Fiber: 7 g
Time: 5 min
Servings: 2

Ingredients
- 2 cup coconut milk or nut milk of choice
- 1 cup chopped organic spinach
- 1 cup chopped organic romaine lettuce or other salad greens
- 1/2-1 avocado, chopped
- 1 tbsp. raw, virgin, and unrefined coconut oil
- 1 tsp. spirulina powder
- 1 tsp. of lemon or lime juice
- 2-3 raw dates, pitted
- additional raw honey to taste

Instructions

1. Add the coconut milk or nut milk to a blender.
2. Add the chopped spinach and lettuce, avocado, coconut oil, spirulina powder, lemon or lime juice, and dates.
3. Blend everything together until smooth.
4. Taste the smoothie and adjust the sweetness as needed with raw honey, if desired.
5. Add a pinch of sea salt and blend briefly to combine.
6. Serve the smoothie cold, over ice if desired. Enjoy!

BROCCOLI GREEN SMOOTHIE

This green smoothie is a great way to start your day with a healthy dose of fiber and vitamin C. The broccoli adds a nice boost of fiber and vitamins, while the banana and pineapple provide natural sweetness and a variety of vitamins and minerals. The almond milk adds a creamy texture and a source of healthy fats, and the optional flax seeds add extra fiber and omega-3 fatty acids. Enjoy this refreshing and nutritious drink as a healthy breakfast or snack!

Calories: 220
Fat: 3 g
Carb: 37 g
Protein: 3 g
Fiber: 5 g
Time: 5 min
Servings: 2

Ingredients

- 3/4 cup broccoli florets, chopped
- 1 banana
- 1/2 cup pineapple chunks
- 1/2 cup almond milk
- 1/2 tsp. flax seeds (optional)

Instructions

1. Add the chopped broccoli, banana, pineapple, and almond milk to a blender.
2. If desired, add the flax seeds to the blender.
3. Blend all the ingredients until smooth and creamy.
4. Pour the smoothie into two glasses and serve immediately.

GINGER PEAR GREEN SMOOTHIE

This green smoothie is a great way to start your day with a boost of energy and nutrients. The pears provide a sweet and juicy flavor, while the ginger adds a spicy kick and has anti-inflammatory properties. The greens add a dose of vitamins and minerals, and the almond milk provides a creamy texture without dairy. This smoothie is a good source of fiber, which can help keep you feeling full and satisfied.

Calories: 165
Fat: 3 g
Carb: 35 g
Protein: 3 g
Fiber: 5 g
Time: 5 min
Servings: 2

Ingredients

- 2 handfuls of greens (spinach, kale, or mixed greens)
- 1 cup almond milk
- 2 large pears, cored and chopped
- 1 inch fresh ginger, peeled and grated

Instructions

1. Wash the greens and chop if necessary.
2. Core and chop the pears.
3. Peel and grate the fresh ginger.
4. Add all the ingredients to a blender and blend until smooth.
5. If the consistency is too thick, add more almond milk until desired consistency is reached.
6. Pour into glasses and enjoy immediately.

BANANA PRUNE GREEN SMOOTHIE

This green smoothie is packed with fiber and natural sweetness from the bananas, prunes, and pear. The almond milk provides a creamy base, while the greens add a boost of nutrients like iron and vitamin C. This smoothie is perfect for a quick and healthy breakfast or snack that will keep you feeling full and energized.

Calories: 236
Fat: 3 g
Carb: 57 g
Protein: 4 g
Fiber: 8 g
Time: 5 min
Servings: 2

Ingredients
- 2 handfuls of greens (such as spinach or kale)
- 2 cups of almond milk
- 2 bananas, peeled and frozen
- 4 prunes, seeded
- 1 pear, cored and chopped

Instructions
1. Add the greens and almond milk to a blender and blend until smooth.
2. Add the frozen bananas, prunes, and chopped pear to the blender and blend until smooth and creamy.
3. If the smoothie is too thick, add more almond milk to thin it out to your desired consistency.
4. Pour into glasses and enjoy!

ORANGE MANGO GREEN SMOOTHIE

This green smoothie is a refreshing and delicious way to start your day. The combination of juicy oranges and sweet mango chunks gives it a tropical flavor, while the greens add a boost of vitamins and minerals. This smoothie is packed with vitamin C, which helps boost the immune system, and fiber, which aids in digestion. It's a great way to sneak some extra greens into your diet and can be enjoyed as a healthy breakfast or snack.

Calories: 121
Fat: 0.5 g
Carb: 31 g
Protein: 2 g
Fiber: 5 g
Time: 5 min
Servings: 2

Ingredients
- 2 handfuls of greens (such as spinach or kale)
- 1 cup of water
- 1 cup of frozen mango chunks
- 2 oranges, peeled and seeded

Instructions
1. Add the greens and water to a blender and blend until smooth.
2. Add the frozen mango chunks and oranges to the blender and blend again until smooth and creamy.
3. If the smoothie is too thick, add more water as needed.
4. Pour into two glasses and enjoy!

GRAPEFRUIT BANANA GREEN SMOOTHIE

This green smoothie is packed with vitamin C from the grapefruit and strawberries, potassium from the banana, and antioxidants from the greens. The stevia provides sweetness without adding any additional calories, making it a healthy and delicious option for a breakfast or snack.

Calories: 260
Fat: 1 g
Carb: 46 g
Protein: 30 g
Fiber: 9 g
Time: 5 min
Servings: 2

- 2 handfuls of greens (such as spinach or kale)
- 1 cup of water
- 1 banana, peeled and frozen
- 1 cup of frozen strawberries
- 1 pink grapefruit, peeled and seeded
- 1 packet of stevia

Ingredients

Instructions

1. Add the greens and water to a blender and blend until smooth.
2. Add the frozen banana and frozen strawberries and blend until smooth.
3. Add the peeled and seeded grapefruit and stevia and blend until smooth.
4. Pour the smoothie into two glasses and enjoy immediately.

ORANGE PLUM GREEN SMOOTHIE

This green smoothie is a delicious and nutritious way to start your day! The combination of oranges and plums provides a good source of vitamin C, while the greens and flaxseeds add a boost of fiber and nutrients. Cinnamon adds a hint of warmth and spice to the smoothie, making it the perfect fall breakfast or snack. Enjoy this smoothie for a quick and easy way to get your daily dose of fruits and veggies!

Calories: 160
Fat: 5 g
Carb: 30 g
Protein: 4 g
Fiber: 9 g
Time: 5 min
Servings: 2

Ingredients
- 2 handfuls of greens (such as spinach or kale)
- 1 cup of ice
- 2 oranges, peeled and seeded
- 1 cup of chopped plums
- 1 teaspoon of cinnamon
- 2 tablespoons of ground flaxseeds

Instructions

1. Add the greens and ice to a blender and blend until the greens are finely chopped.
2. Add the oranges, plums, cinnamon, and flaxseeds to the blender.
3. Pour in enough water to cover the ingredients and blend until smooth and creamy.
4. If the smoothie is too thick, add more water until it reaches the desired consistency.
5. Pour into glasses and enjoy!

ORANGE BERRY SEEDS SMOOTHIE

This Orange Berry Seeds smoothie is a delicious and nutritious way to start your day. Packed with vitamin C from the orange and mixed berries, as well as antioxidants from the goji berries and ground flaxseeds, this smoothie is a great source of energy and nutrients. The plant-based protein powder adds extra protein to keep you feeling full and satisfied throughout the morning. Enjoy this smoothie as a healthy breakfast or snack any time of day.

Calories: 260
Fat: 6 g
Carb: 40 g
Protein: 18 g
Fiber: 11 g
Time: 5 min
Servings: 2

Ingredients

- 2 handfuls of greens (spinach or kale)
- 1 cup unsweetened almond milk
- 1 small orange, peeled
- 1 cup frozen mixed berries
- 1 teaspoon goji berries, soaked for 5 minutes
- 1 tablespoon ground flaxseeds
- 1 scoop of plant-based protein powder

Instructions

1. Add the greens and almond milk to a blender and blend until smooth.
2. Add the orange, mixed berries, goji berries, ground flaxseeds, and protein powder to the blender and blend until smooth.
3. If the smoothie is too thick, add more almond milk to thin it out to your desired consistency.
4. Pour into glasses and enjoy!

MINTY PEAR GREEN SMOOTHIE

This minty pear green smoothie is a refreshing and nutrient-dense drink that is perfect for breakfast or as a snack. Pears are a great source of fiber, vitamin C, and copper, while the ginger adds a zingy kick and may help with digestion. The fresh mint leaves not only provide a refreshing flavor but also contain antioxidants and may aid in digestion as well. The mixed greens add a boost of vitamins and minerals, making this smoothie a great way to start your day on a healthy note.

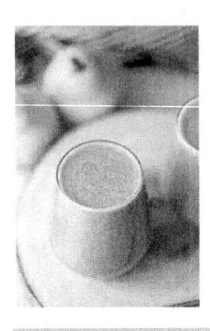

Calories: 121
Fat: 1 g
Carb: 31 g
Protein: 2 g
Fiber: 7 g
Time: 5 min
Servings: 2

Ingredients
- 2 handfuls of mixed greens (spinach, kale, or chard)
- 1 cup of water
- 2 pears, peeled and cored
- ¼-inch section of fresh ginger, grated
- ¼ cup chopped fresh mint leaves

Instructions

1. Add the mixed greens and water to a blender and blend until smooth.
2. Add the pears, grated ginger, and chopped mint leaves to the blender and blend until smooth.
3. If the smoothie is too thick, add more water until it reaches your desired consistency.

PEACHY MANGO GREEN SMOOTHIE

This Peachy Mango Green Smoothie is packed with flavor and nutrition. Arugula adds a peppery kick while the sweet and juicy combination of peaches, nectarines, mango, and plums make this smoothie a refreshing treat. Plus, it's high in fiber and contains no added sugar, making it a healthy choice for breakfast or a snack.

Calories: 165
Fat: 1 g
Carb: 41 g
Protein: 33 g
Fiber: 7 g
Time: 5 min
Servings: 2

Ingredients
- 2 handfuls arugula
- 1 cup water
- 2 cups frozen peaches
- 2 nectarines, peeled, cored, and seeded
- 1 cup frozen mango chunks
- 2 plums, cored and seeded

Instructions
1. Add the arugula and water to a blender and blend until smooth.
2. Add the frozen peaches, nectarines, mango chunks, and plums to the blender and blend until smooth.
3. If the smoothie is too thick, add more water until you reach your desired consistency.
4. Pour the smoothie into two glasses and enjoy!

COCONUT BERRIES GREEN SMOOTHIE

This green smoothie is a great source of antioxidants from the goji berries and nectarines, as well as fiber from the greens and shredded coconut. It also contains healthy fats from the coconut and is a good source of potassium from the banana. It's a delicious and healthy way to start your day!

Calories: 190
Fat: 6 g
Carb: 53 g
Protein: 4 g
Fiber: 12 g
Time: 5 min
Servings: 2

- 2 handfuls of greens (spinach or kale)
- 1 cup of water
- 2 nectarines, peeled, cored, and seeded
- 1 frozen banana, peeled
- 1/2 cup of goji berries
- 1/4 cup of shredded coconut

Ingredients

Instructions

1. Add the greens and water to a blender and blend until smooth.
2. Add the nectarines, banana, goji berries, and shredded coconut to the blender and blend until smooth.
3. If the smoothie is too thick, add more water until you reach the desired consistency.
4. Pour the smoothie into glasses and enjoy.

SUNFLOWER ORANGE GREEN SMOOTHIE

This green smoothie is a great source of vitamin C from the oranges and grapes, as well as fiber from the arugula and ground flaxseeds. The addition of sunflower oil provides healthy fats and helps to keep you feeling full and satisfied. Enjoy this refreshing and nutritious drink as a healthy breakfast or snack.

Calories: 299
Fat: 18 g
Carb: 36 g
Protein: 5 g
Fiber: 8 g
Time: 5 min
Servings: 2

Ingredients
- 2 cups arugula
- 1 cup water
- 2 oranges, peeled and seeded
- 1 cup red grapes
- 2 tablespoons ground flaxseeds
- 2 tablespoons sunflower oil

Instructions
1. Add the arugula and water to a blender and blend until smooth.
2. Add the oranges, grapes, ground flaxseeds, and sunflower oil to the blender and blend until smooth and creamy.
3. Pour the smoothie into glasses and serve immediately.

AVOCADO APPLE SMOOTHIE

This Avocado Apple smoothie is a great source of vitamins and minerals, such as vitamin C, potassium, and iron. The avocado adds healthy fats and creaminess, while the beets and cacao powder provide antioxidants and nutrients. This smoothie is a delicious and nutritious way to start your day or to enjoy as a refreshing snack.

Calories: 308
Fat: 17 g
Carb: 43 g
Protein: 4 g
Fiber: 13 g
Time: 5 min
Servings: 2

Ingredients
- 2 handfuls of greens (spinach, kale, or mixed greens)
- 1 cup unsweetened apple juice
- 1 cup ice
- 2 small apples, cored and seeded
- 1 avocado, peeled and cored
- 1/4 cup beets, peeled and diced
- 1 tablespoon cacao powder

Instructions

1. Wash the greens and chop them if needed.
2. Add the greens, apple juice, and ice to a blender.
3. Blend until smooth.
4. Add the apples, avocado, beets, and cacao powder to the blender.
5. Blend until smooth and creamy.
6. Pour the smoothie into two glasses and serve immediately.

ORANGE APRICOT GREEN SMOOTHIE

This green smoothie is a great source of vitamin C from the oranges and a good source of fiber from the apricots and arugula. The almond butter and almonds add healthy fats and protein to keep you feeling full and satisfied. It's a delicious and nutritious way to start your day or enjoy as a snack.

Calories: 465
Fat: 30 g
Carb: 44 g
Protein: 12 g
Fiber: 11 g
Time: 5 min
Servings: 2

Ingredients
- 2 handfuls arugula
- 1 cup water
- 2 oranges, peeled and seeded
- 6 dried apricots, pitted
- 1 banana, peeled and frozen
- 1/2 cup almonds
- 1/4 cup almond butter

Instructions

1. Add the arugula and water to a blender and blend until smooth.
2. Add the oranges, dried apricots, frozen banana, almonds, and almond butter to the blender and blend until smooth and creamy.
3. If the smoothie is too thick, add more water until it reaches your desired consistency.
4. Pour into two glasses and enjoy!

CHOCOLATEY AND NUTTY GREEN SMOOTHIE

This green smoothie is a great source of plant-based protein and healthy fats from the cashews, as well as fiber from the greens and dates. The raw cacao powder provides a rich chocolate flavor and is also high in antioxidants. Stevia is used as a natural sweetener without adding any calories or sugar. Enjoy as a healthy dessert or snack!

Calories: 294
Fat: 22 g
Carb: 38 g
Protein: 9 g
Fiber: 7 g
Time: 5 min
Servings: 2

Ingredients
- 2 handfuls of greens (spinach or kale)
- 2 cups of water
- 1 cup of cashew nuts
- 1/4 cup of raw cacao powder
- 6 large pitted dates
- 1 packet of stevia

Instructions
1. Add the greens and water to a blender and blend until smooth.
2. Add the cashew nuts, cacao powder, dates, and stevia to the blender and blend until smooth and creamy.
3. If the mixture is too thick, add more water until desired consistency is reached.
4. Pour into glasses and enjoy!

BERRY MEDLEY GREEN SMOOTHIE

This green smoothie is packed with antioxidants and fiber from the mixed berries and mixed greens. The cashew milk adds a creamy texture and nutty flavor, while the dates provide natural sweetness. The vanilla extract gives it a delicious aroma and flavor. It's a healthy and refreshing drink that can be enjoyed for breakfast, as a snack, or even as a dessert.

Calories: 94
Fat: 3 g
Carb: 45 g
Protein: 5 g
Fiber: 11 g
Time: 5 min
Servings: 2

Ingredients

- 2 handfuls of mixed greens
- 2 cups of unsweetened cashew milk
- 2 cups of frozen mixed berries
- 2 large pitted dates
- 2 teaspoons of vanilla extract

Instructions

1. Start by adding the mixed greens and cashew milk to a blender. Blend on high until the greens are fully pureed.
2. Add the frozen mixed berries, pitted dates, and vanilla extract to the blender.
3. Blend again on high until the mixture is smooth and creamy.
4. Pour the smoothie into two glasses and enjoy!

CELERY AVOCADO GREEN SMOOTHIE

This green smoothie is a good source of healthy fats from avocado and fiber from celery and cucumber. Mint adds a refreshing taste while also aiding digestion. Enjoy it as a healthy breakfast or snack to start your day off right.

Calories: 178
Fat: 16 g
Carb: 11 g
Protein: 3 g
Fiber: 7 g
Time: 5 min
Servings: 2

Ingredients
- 1 stalk of celery
- 1 avocado
- 1/2 fresh cucumber
- A handful of fresh mint leaves
- 1 cup of water or coconut water (for desired consistency)

Instructions

1. Wash and chop the celery, avocado, and cucumber into small pieces.
2. Add them into a blender along with the fresh mint leaves.
3. Add the water or coconut water and blend until smooth.
4. If needed, add more water or coconut water to achieve your desired consistency.
5. Pour the smoothie into glasses and enjoy!

GREEN SMOOTHIE WITH CELERY CUCUMBER SPINACH

This green smoothie is packed with nutrient-rich ingredients, including celery, cucumbers, spinach, lettuce, and ginger. The mineral water helps to thin out the smoothie and provides a refreshing, hydrating base. This smoothie is low in calories, high in fiber, and rich in vitamins and minerals. It's a great way to start your day or to enjoy as a healthy snack.

Calories: 44
Fat: 21g
Carb: 9 g
Protein: 3 g
Fiber: 3 g
Time: 5 min
Servings: 2

Ingredients
- 2-3 stalks of celery
- 2 medium cucumbers
- 1 bunch of baby spinach
- 1 bunch of lettuce leaves
- 2 cm of fresh ginger root
- Mineral water

Instructions

1. Rinse all the vegetables thoroughly.
2. Chop the celery, cucumbers, and ginger into small pieces.
3. Add the chopped vegetables, baby spinach, and lettuce leaves into a blender.
4. Pour in enough mineral water to cover the vegetables in the blender.
5. Blend until the mixture is smooth and creamy.
6. Pour the green smoothie into glasses and serve immediately.

CELERY APPLE DETOX GREEN SMOOTHIE

This green smoothie is a great way to get a boost of vitamins and nutrients in the morning. The celery provides a subtle, refreshing flavor and is a good source of antioxidants, while the green apples add natural sweetness and are rich in vitamin C. The spinach is packed with iron and fiber, and the lemon juice adds a zesty kick of vitamin C. This smoothie is a great way to start the day on a healthy note.

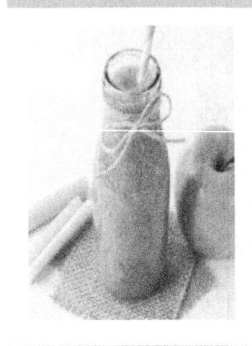

Calories: 105
Fat: 0 g
Carb: 27 g
Protein: 2 g
Fiber: 6 g
Time: 5 min
Servings: 2

Ingredients
- 1 celery stalk
- 2 large green apples, cored and chopped
- 2 cups fresh or frozen spinach
- 1/2 lemon, juiced
- 1/2 cup water or ice (optional)

Instructions
1. Add the celery, green apples, spinach, and lemon juice to a blender.
2. Pour in the water and blend until smooth. If the mixture is too thick, add more water to achieve the desired consistency.
3. Pour the smoothie into two glasses and enjoy immediately.

GREEN SMOOTHIE WITH CELERY AND PARSLEY

This green smoothie is a refreshing and nutritious drink that can be enjoyed as a healthy breakfast or snack. The celery provides a good source of vitamin K, while the parsley is a great source of vitamin C and vitamin A. The cucumber adds hydration and natural sweetness, and the ginger and lemon provide a zesty kick. The apple juice adds extra sweetness and helps to blend all the flavors together. Overall, this smoothie is packed with vitamins and antioxidants to help you feel your best!

Calories: 70
Fat: 0,6g
Carb: 17 g
Protein: 2 g
Fiber: 2 g
Time: 5 min
Servings: 2

Ingredients
- 2 celery stalks
- 1/2 cup fresh parsley leaves
- 1 medium cucumber
- 1 cup unsweetened apple juice
- 1 inch fresh ginger root
- Juice of 1/2 lemon

Instructions

1. Wash all the ingredients thoroughly.
2. Cut the celery and cucumber into small pieces.
3. Peel the ginger root and chop it into small pieces.
4. Add all the ingredients to a blender.
5. Blend until smooth.
6. If the smoothie is too thick, add some water or more apple juice to thin it out.
7. Pour into glasses and enjoy!

AVOCADO CABBAGE SPINACH GREEN SMOOTHIE

This smoothie is rich in healthy fats from the avocado, as well as vitamins A, C, and K from the kale and spinach. It also contains fiber and protein. The nutritional values may vary depending on the size of the ingredients used.

Calories: 190
Fat: 20 g
Carb: 18 g
Protein: 5 g
Fiber: 11 g
Time: 5 min
Servings: 2

Ingredients
- 1 ripe avocado
- 2 cups chopped kale leaves
- 2 cups fresh spinach leaves
- 2 cups water

Instructions

1. Add the avocado, kale, and spinach to a blender.
2. Pour in the water and blend until smooth and creamy.
3. Pour the smoothie into two glasses and enjoy immediately.

PEANUT BUTTER-STRAWBERRY-KALE SMOOTHIE

This green smoothie is a delicious and nutritious combination of creamy soy milk, sweet strawberries, and nutrient-rich kale. The addition of peanut butter adds protein and healthy fats, while the honey and vanilla extract provide a touch of sweetness and flavor. It's a refreshing and satisfying drink that can be enjoyed as a healthy breakfast or snack.

Calories: 185
Fat: 7 g
Carb: 37 g
Protein: 10 g
Fiber: 6 g
Time: 5 min
Servings: 2

Ingredients
- 1 cup unsweetened soy milk
- 1 cup frozen strawberries
- 1 cup chopped kale
- 1 tablespoon natural peanut butter
- 1 tablespoon honey
- 1 teaspoon vanilla extract
- 2-4 ice cubes

Instructions

1. In a blender, combine the soy milk, frozen strawberries, chopped kale, peanut butter, honey, vanilla extract, and ice cubes.
2. Blend on high speed until smooth and creamy.
3. If the smoothie is too thick, add more soy milk to reach your desired consistency.

PINEAPPLE-GRAPEFRUIT DETOX SMOOTHIE

This green smoothie is a refreshing and hydrating blend of coconut water, tropical pineapple, nutrient-rich spinach, tangy grapefruit, and zesty ginger. It's packed with vitamins, minerals, and antioxidants to support your overall health. The smoothie provides a balance of flavors and textures, making it a delicious and nutritious choice for a breakfast or snack. Enjoy its vibrant taste and feel refreshed!

Calories: 145
Fat: 0 g
Carb: 36 g
Protein: 2 g
Fiber: 5 g
Time: 5 min
Servings: 2

Ingredients
- 1 cup plain coconut water
- 1 cup frozen diced pineapple
- 1 cup packed baby spinach
- 1 small grapefruit, peeled and segmented, plus any juice squeezed from the membranes
- ½ teaspoon grated fresh ginger
- 1 cup ice

Instructions

1. In a blender, combine the coconut water, frozen pineapple, baby spinach, grapefruit segments and juice, grated ginger, and ice.
2. Blend on high speed until smooth and creamy.
3. If the smoothie is too thick, add more coconut water to reach your desired consistency.

ALOE SMOOTHIE

This green smoothie is a tropical delight packed with the goodness of pineapple, mango, kale, coconut milk, aloe vera gel, and ginger. It's a refreshing and nutritious blend that provides vitamins, minerals, antioxidants, and fiber to support your well-being. The optional chia seeds add an extra boost of nutrients. Enjoy this vibrant and healthy smoothie as a breakfast or snack, and feel energized throughout the day!

Calories: 145
Fat: 5 g
Carb: 45 g
Protein: 3 g
Fiber: 7 g
Time: 5 min
Servings: 2

- 1 cup fresh or frozen diced pineapple
- 1 cup fresh or frozen diced mango
- 1 cup chopped kale
- 1 cup chilled coconut milk beverage
- 2 tablespoons pure aloe vera gel
- 1 teaspoon grated fresh ginger
- Chia seeds (optional)

Ingredients

Instructions

1. In a blender, combine the pineapple, mango, kale, coconut milk, aloe vera gel, and grated ginger.
2. Blend on high speed until smooth and creamy.
3. If desired, add chia seeds for extra fiber and omega-3 fatty acids. Start with 1 tablespoon and adjust to your preference.
4. Pour the smoothie into two glasses and serve immediately.

GREEN PIÑA COLADA SMOOTHIE

This green smoothie is a nutritious and satisfying blend of Greek yogurt, pineapple, leafy greens, coconut milk, and vanilla extract. It provides a good amount of protein from the Greek yogurt, vitamins and minerals from the pineapple and greens, and a creamy touch from the coconut milk. The optional chia seeds add extra fiber and healthy fats. Top it off with some unsweetened coconut flakes for a tropical twist. Enjoy this refreshing smoothie as a healthy breakfast or snack to start your day on a nutritious note!

Calories: 220
Fat: 4 g
Carb: 31 g
Protein: 17 g
Fiber: 5 g
Time: 5 min
Servings: 2

Ingredients
- 1 cup nonfat plain Greek yogurt
- 1 cup frozen pineapple
- 1 cup kale or baby spinach
- ½ cup "lite" coconut milk
- ½ teaspoon vanilla extract
- Unsweetened coconut flakes for garnish
- Chia seeds (optional)

Instructions

1. In a blender, combine the Greek yogurt, frozen pineapple, kale or baby spinach, coconut milk, and vanilla extract.
2. Blend on high speed until smooth and creamy.
3. If desired, add chia seeds for additional fiber and omega-3 fatty acids. Start with 1 tablespoon and adjust to your preference.
4. Pour the smoothie into two glasses and garnish with unsweetened coconut flakes.
5. Serve and enjoy!

CREAMY ZUCCHINI SMOOTHIE

This green smoothie is packed with nutritious ingredients. The frozen zucchini and banana provide a creamy base while adding vitamins and minerals. The peanut butter adds a delicious nutty flavor and a dose of healthy fats and protein. You can sweeten the smoothie with either honey or Medjool dates for a natural touch of sweetness. The optional addition of fresh baby spinach increases the nutrient content, including iron and folate. Enjoy this green smoothie as a satisfying and energizing breakfast or snack!

Calories: 220
Fat: 11 g
Carb: 29 g
Protein: 6 g
Fiber: 5 g
Time: 5 min
Servings: 2

Ingredients
- 1 cup water
- 1 cup frozen zucchini
- 1 frozen banana, cut into coins
- 2 tablespoons peanut butter
- 1 teaspoon honey (or substitute with 2 pitted Medjool dates)
- 1 handful fresh baby spinach (optional)

Instructions
1. In a blender, add the water, frozen zucchini, frozen banana, peanut butter, honey (or dates), and baby spinach (if using).
2. Blend on high speed until smooth and creamy.
3. If the consistency is too thick, you can add more water as needed to reach your desired consistency.
4. Pour the smoothie into two glasses and serve.

GREEN GRAPES SMOOTHIE

This green smoothie is a refreshing and nutritious drink. Green grapes add natural sweetness and antioxidants, while spinach or green lettuce provide vitamins, minerals, and fiber. The addition of orange juice not only enhances the flavor but also contributes to the vitamin C content. Enjoy this green smoothie as a healthy way to boost your fruit and vegetable intake and start your day on a nutritious note!

Calories: 120
Fat: 0 g
Carb: 29 g
Protein: 2 g
Fiber: 6 g
Time: 5 min
Servings: 2

Ingredients
- 1 cup green grapes
- 1 cup spinach or green lettuce
  1 cup orange juice

-

Instructions

1. Wash the green grapes, spinach or green lettuce thoroughly.
2. In a blender, add the green grapes, spinach or green lettuce, and orange juice.
3. Blend on high speed until smooth and well combined.
4. If the consistency is too thick, you can add more orange juice to reach your desired consistency.
5. Pour the smoothie into two glasses and serve.

SUPER HEALTHY SMOOTHIE

This green smoothie is a healthy and nutritious drink. The celery provides a refreshing and slightly tangy flavor, while the banana adds natural sweetness and creaminess. The carrot adds a hint of sweetness and a boost of beta-carotene. The yogurt adds creaminess and provides protein and calcium. Enjoy this green smoothie as a satisfying and nourishing snack or breakfast option to start your day off right.

Calories: 170
Fat: 2 g
Carb: 34 g
Protein: 8 g
Fiber: 5 g
Time: 5 min
Servings: 2

Ingredients
- 1 cup chopped celery stalk
- 1 banana
- 1 carrot
- 1 cup yogurt

Instructions

1. Wash and chop the celery stalk, peel and slice the banana, and peel and chop the carrot.
2. In a blender, add the chopped celery, banana slices, carrot pieces, and yogurt.
3. Blend on high speed until smooth and well combined.
4. If the consistency is too thick, you can add a splash of water or more yogurt to adjust it to your liking.

GREEN SMOOTHIE WITH OATMEAL AND FLAX

This green smoothie is packed with nutritious ingredients. The celery, spinach, and parsley provide vitamins, minerals, and antioxidants. The oat flakes and flaxseed add fiber and healthy fats. The cucumber adds hydration and a refreshing taste. The lemon juice adds a tangy flavor, while the olive oil provides healthy monounsaturated fats. Enjoy this green smoothie as a wholesome and energizing drink that supports your overall well-being.

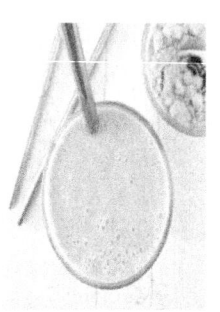

Calories: 200
Fat: 12 g
Carb: 18 g
Protein: 6 g
Fiber: 6 g
Time: 5 min
Servings: 2

Ingredients
- 2-3 stalks of celery
- 50g spinach
- 50g parsley
- 3 tbsp oat flakes
- 1 tbsp flaxseed
- 2-3 tbsp olive oil
- 300g drinking water
- 200g cucumber
- 1 tbsp lemon juice
- Sea salt to taste

Instructions

1. Wash the celery stalks, spinach, parsley, and cucumber.
2. Chop the celery stalks, spinach, parsley, and cucumber into smaller pieces for easier blending.
3. In a blender, add the chopped celery, spinach, parsley, cucumber, oat flakes, flaxseed, olive oil, lemon juice, and a pinch of sea salt.
4. Blend on high speed until the ingredients are well combined and smooth.
5. If the consistency is too thick, you can add more water and blend again.
6. Taste the smoothie and adjust the seasoning if needed by adding more lemon juice or sea salt.
7. Pour the smoothie into two glasses and serve chilled.

LETTUCE AND GINGER DETOX SMOOTHIE

This green smoothie is a refreshing and nutritious blend. The coconut water provides hydration and natural sweetness, while the Romaine lettuce adds vitamins and minerals. The banana adds creaminess and natural sweetness, while the ginger tea adds a hint of warmth and flavor. The key lime juice adds tanginess and brightness, and the blueberries provide antioxidants and a burst of color. Enjoy this green smoothie as a revitalizing and healthy drink to start your day or as a refreshing snack.

Calories: 160
Fat: 1 g
Carb: 37 g
Protein: 2 g
Fiber: 5 g
Time: 5 min
Servings: 2

Ingredients
- 1 cup of coconut water
- 2 cups chopped Romaine lettuce
- 1 small banana, peeled
- 1 cup ginger tea, cooled
- 6 tablespoons key lime juice
- ½ cup whole blueberries, fresh

Instructions

1. Take a high-powered blender, switch it on, and then place all the ingredients inside, in order.
2. Cover the blender with its lid and then pulse at high speed for 1 minute or more until smooth.
3. Distribute the smoothie between two glasses and then serve.

KALE AND GINGER GREEN SMOOTHIE

This green smoothie is packed with nutrients and provides a refreshing and healthy blend. The kale leaves offer a rich source of vitamins and minerals, while the fresh apple adds natural sweetness and fiber. The ginger adds a hint of spice and promotes digestion, and the cucumber provides hydration and a refreshing taste. The key lime juice adds tanginess and brightness to the smoothie, while the sea moss gel offers additional minerals and nutrients. Enjoy this green smoothie as a nutritious and revitalizing drink to start your day or as a refreshing snack.

Calories: 67
Fat: 0 g
Carb: 15 g
Protein: 1 g
Fiber: 3 g
Time: 5 min
Servings: 2

Ingredients
- 2 cups spring water
- 1 cup kale leaves, fresh
- ¼ cup key lime juice
- 1 medium fresh apple, cored
- 1-inch piece of ginger, fresh
- 1 cup sliced cucumber, fresh
- 1 tablespoon of sea moss gel

Instructions

1. In a blender, combine the spring water, kale leaves, key lime juice, fresh apple, ginger, cucumber, and sea moss gel.
2. Blend on high speed until all the ingredients are well combined and smooth.
3. If the consistency is too thick, you can add more water and blend again.
4. Taste the smoothie and adjust the flavor by adding more key lime juice or sweetener if desired.
5. Pour the smoothie into two glasses and serve chilled.

ARUGULA AND CUCUMBER SMOOTHIE

This green smoothie is a vibrant and nutritious blend packed with fresh ingredients. Callaloo and arugula provide a variety of vitamins and minerals, while cucumber and honeydew contribute hydration and a refreshing taste. Ginger adds a touch of spice and aids digestion, and the pear and Medjool dates add natural sweetness and fiber. Lime juice adds tanginess and brightness to the smoothie, and the sea moss gel provides additional minerals and nutrients. Enjoy this invigorating green smoothie as a nourishing way to start your day or as a refreshing pick-me-up.

Calories: 150
Fat: 1 g
Carb: 38 g
Protein: 4 g
Fiber: 8 g
Time: 5 min
Servings: 2

Ingredients
- 2 cups of spring water
- 1 large bunch of callaloo, fresh
- 1/4 cup of lime juice
- 1 cup diced cucumber, fresh
- 1 large bunch of arugula, fresh
- 1/4 of a honeydew, fresh
- 1-inch piece of ginger, fresh
- 1 pear, destemmed, diced
- 6 Medjool dates, pitted
- 1 tablespoon of sea moss gel

Instructions
1. In a blender, combine the spring water, callaloo, lime juice, diced cucumber, arugula, honeydew, ginger, pear, dates, and sea moss gel.
2. Blend on high speed until all the ingredients are well combined and smooth.
3. If the consistency is too thick, you can add more water and blend again.
4. Taste the smoothie and adjust the flavor by adding more lime juice or sweetener if desired.
5. Pour the smoothie into two glasses and serve chilled.

DANDELION AND WATERCRESS SMOOTHIE

This green smoothie is a refreshing and nutrient-rich blend. Dandelion greens and watercress provide a wealth of vitamins and minerals, while bananas and blueberries add natural sweetness and antioxidants. Ginger adds a hint of spiciness and aids digestion, while Medjool dates provide additional natural sweetness and fiber. The key lime juice adds tanginess and brightness to the smoothie. Burdock root powder adds a touch of earthiness and offers potential health benefits. Enjoy this invigorating green smoothie as a nourishing way to boost your energy and support your well-being.

Calories: 180
Fat: 1 g
Carb: 45 g
Protein: 3 g
Fiber: 9 g
Time: 5 min
Servings: 2

Ingredients
- 2 cups spring water
- 1 large bunch of dandelion greens, fresh
- 1/4 cup key lime juice
- 1 cup watercress, fresh
- 3 baby bananas, peeled
- 1/2 cup fresh blueberries
- 1-inch piece of ginger, fresh
- 6 Medjool dates, pitted
- 1 tablespoon burdock root powder

Instructions

1. In a blender, combine the spring water, dandelion greens, key lime juice, watercress, baby bananas, blueberries, ginger, Medjool dates, and burdock root powder.
2. Blend on high speed until all the ingredients are well combined and smooth.
3. If the consistency is too thick, you can add more water and blend again.
4. Taste the smoothie and adjust the flavor by adding more lime juice or sweetener if desired.
5. Pour the smoothie into two glasses and serve chilled.

LETTUCE AND ORANGE SMOOTHIE

This green smoothie is a refreshing and nourishing blend. The coconut water provides hydration and natural sweetness, while the lettuce leaves offer a boost of vitamins and minerals. The key lime and Seville orange add a tangy and citrusy flavor to the smoothie. The bromide plus powder adds an additional nutritional boost. The avocado adds a creamy texture and healthy fats to the smoothie. Enjoy this green smoothie as a delicious and nutritious way to start your day or recharge your energy.

Calories: 150
Fat: 7 g
Carb: 19 g
Protein: 2 g
Fiber: 7 g
Time: 5 min
Servings: 2

Ingredients
- 1 cup coconut water
- 1 cup lettuce leaves, fresh
- Juice of 1 key lime
- 1 Seville orange, peeled
- 1 tablespoon bromide plus powder
- 1/2 medium avocado, pitted

Instructions
1. In a blender, combine the coconut water, lettuce leaves, key lime juice, peeled Seville orange, bromide plus powder, and avocado.
2. Blend on high speed until all the ingredients are well combined and smooth.
3. If the consistency is too thick, you can add more coconut water and blend again.
4. Taste the smoothie and adjust the flavor by adding more lime juice or sweetener if desired.
5. Pour the smoothie into two glasses and serve chilled.

BERRIES AND HEMP SEEDS SMOOTHIE

This green smoothie is packed with nutrients and flavor. The fresh lettuce adds a vibrant green color and a dose of vitamins and minerals. The banana provides natural sweetness and a creamy texture. The mixed berries add a burst of antioxidants and natural sweetness. The Seville orange contributes a tangy and citrusy flavor. The hemp seeds provide plant-based protein and healthy fats. The avocado adds creaminess and additional healthy fats. Enjoy this green smoothie as a refreshing and nutritious way to start your day or as a satisfying snack.

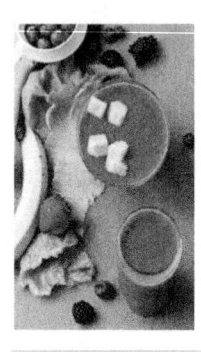

Calories: 220
Fat: 10 g
Carb: 31 g
Protein: 6 g
Fiber: 9 g
Time: 5 min
Servings: 2

Ingredients
- 1 cup spring water
- 2 cups fresh lettuce
- 1 medium banana, peeled
- 1 cup mixed berries, fresh
- 1 Seville orange, peeled
- 1 tablespoon hemp seeds
- 1/4 avocado, pitted
-

Instructions

1. In a blender, add the spring water, fresh lettuce, peeled banana, mixed berries, peeled Seville orange, hemp seeds, and avocado.
2. Blend on high speed until all the ingredients are well combined and smooth.
3. If the consistency is too thick, you can add more water and blend again.
4. Taste the smoothie and adjust the flavor by adding more orange juice or sweetener if desired.

PEAR, BERRIES, AND QUINOA SMOOTHIE

This green smoothie is a nutritious and filling option. The avocado adds creaminess and healthy fats, while the pears provide natural sweetness and fiber. The cooked quinoa adds a source of plant-based protein and additional fiber. The blueberries contribute antioxidants and a burst of flavor. The spinach adds a dose of vitamins and minerals. Enjoy this green smoothie as a nourishing breakfast or a refreshing snack to fuel your day.

Calories: 250
Fat: 9 g
Carb: 42 g
Protein: 7 g
Fiber: 10 g
Time: 5 min
Servings: 2

Ingredients
- 2 cups spring water
- 1/2 avocado, pitted
- 2 fresh pears, chopped
- 1/2 cup cooked quinoa
- 1/4 cup fresh whole blueberries
- 1 handful fresh baby spinach (optional)

Instructions

1. In a blender, add the spring water, avocado, chopped pears, cooked quinoa, fresh blueberries, and spinach.
2. Blend on high speed until all the ingredients are well combined and smooth.
3. If the consistency is too thick, you can add more water and blend again.
4. Taste the smoothie and adjust the flavor by adding more fruit or sweetener if desired.
5. Pour the smoothie into two glasses and serve chilled.

BERRIES AND SEA MOSS SMOOTHIE

This green smoothie is a refreshing and hydrating option. The coconut water provides electrolytes and natural sweetness. The lettuce leaves add a boost of vitamins and minerals. The banana contributes creaminess and potassium. The mixed berries offer antioxidants and natural sweetness. The sea moss adds a nutritional boost with its high mineral content. The key lime juice adds a tangy flavor. Enjoy this green smoothie as a nutritious and delicious way to start your day or recharge in the afternoon.

Calories: 150
Fat: 11 g
Carb: 35 g
Protein: 3 g
Fiber: 7 g
Time: 5 min
Servings: 2

Ingredients
- 1 cup coconut water
- 2 cups lettuce leaves
- 1 banana, peeled
- 1 cup mixed berries (such as strawberries, blueberries, raspberries)
- 1 tablespoon sea moss
- Juice of 2 key limes

Instructions

1. In a blender, add the coconut water, lettuce leaves, peeled banana, mixed berries, sea moss, and key lime juice.
2. Blend on high speed until all the ingredients are well combined and smooth.
3. If the consistency is too thick, you can add more coconut water or water and blend again.
4. Taste the smoothie and adjust the flavor by adding more lime juice or sweetener if desired.

RASPBERRY AND CHARD SMOOTHIE

This green smoothie is packed with nutrients and refreshing flavors. The coconut water provides hydration and natural sweetness. The Swiss chard leaves are rich in vitamins and minerals, including vitamin K and iron. The key lime juice adds a tangy twist and a boost of vitamin C. The fresh raspberries offer antioxidants and fiber. Enjoy this green smoothie as a healthy and energizing option for breakfast or as a refreshing pick-me-up throughout the day.

Calories: 120
Fat: 1 g
Carb: 298g
Protein: 4 g
Fiber: 10 g
Time: 5 min
Servings: 2

Ingredients
- 2 cups of coconut water
- 2 cups Swiss chard leaves
- Juice of 2 key limes
- 2 cups fresh whole raspberries

Instructions

1. In a blender, add the coconut water, Swiss chard leaves, key lime juice, and fresh raspberries.
2. Blend on high speed until all the ingredients are well combined and smooth.
3. If the consistency is too thick, you can add more coconut water and blend again.
4. Taste the smoothie and adjust the flavor by adding more lime juice if desired.
5. Pour the smoothie into two glasses and serve chilled.

BANANA, BERRY, AND KALE SMOOTHIE

This green smoothie is a nutritious and refreshing blend of strawberries, bananas, kale, and ice. Strawberries add a sweet and tangy flavor while providing vitamin C and antioxidants. Bananas contribute creaminess and additional natural sweetness, along with potassium and fiber. Kale, a leafy green, adds a boost of vitamins A, K, and C, as well as fiber. The smoothie is a great way to incorporate greens into your diet and enjoy a refreshing drink packed with essential nutrients. It can be enjoyed as a healthy breakfast, post-workout snack, or anytime you need a revitalizing boost.

Calories: 180
Fat: 1 g
Carb: 43 g
Protein: 4 g
Fiber: 9 g
Time: 5 min
Servings: 2

Ingredients
- 2 cups fresh whole strawberries
- 2 bananas, peeled
- 2 cups chopped kale
- 1 cup of ice cubes

Instructions

1. Place all the ingredients in a blender.
2. Blend on high speed until the mixture is smooth and well combined.
3. If the consistency is too thick, you can add a little water or more ice cubes and blend again.
4. Taste the smoothie and adjust the sweetness by adding more strawberries or bananas if desired.
5. Pour the smoothie into two glasses and serve chilled.

CUCUMBER AND COCONUT SMOOTHIE

This green smoothie is a refreshing and hydrating blend of coconut water, Swiss chard, cucumber, lime, date, and ginger. Coconut water provides natural sweetness and electrolytes, while Swiss chard adds a dose of vitamins A, K, and C, as well as minerals. Cucumber contributes hydration and a refreshing taste, while lime adds a tangy kick and vitamin C. The Medjool date adds natural sweetness and fiber, and ginger adds a hint of spice and potential health benefits. This smoothie is a great way to incorporate greens and hydrating ingredients into your diet, providing a refreshing and nutritious drink. Enjoy it as a healthy breakfast, snack, or post-workout refresher.

Calories: 90
Fat: 0 g
Carb: 20 g
Protein: 3 g
Fiber: 4 g
Time: 5 min
Servings: 2

Ingredients
- 2 cups coconut water
- 2 cups Swiss chards, fresh
- 1 large cucumber, peeled
- 1 key lime, peeled
- 1 Medjool date, pitted
- 1-inch piece of ginger, fresh

Instructions

1. Add all the ingredients to a blender.
2. Blend on high speed until the mixture is smooth and well combined.
3. If the consistency is too thick, you can add a little more coconut water and blend again.
4. Taste the smoothie and adjust the sweetness or tanginess by adding more lime juice or date if desired.

SAGE BLACKBERRY SMOOTHIE

This green smoothie combines the sweetness of blackberries, apple, and pear with the refreshing flavor of basil. Cashews add creaminess and a source of healthy fats, while water and ice create a smooth texture. Blackberries are rich in antioxidants, while apples and pears provide vitamins and fiber. Basil adds a touch of herbaceousness and potential health benefits. This smoothie is a delicious and nutritious way to enjoy a blend of fruits, nuts, and herbs. It can be enjoyed as a refreshing breakfast, snack, or post-workout drink.

Calories: 170
Fat: 7 g
Carb: 25 g
Protein: 4 g
Fiber: 6 g
Time: 5 min
Servings: 2

Ingredients
- 1 oz. blackberries
- 4 oz. apple
- 1 pear, chopped
- 3 basil leaves
- 3 tbsp. cashews
- 1 cup water
- 1 cup ice

Instructions
1. Add all the ingredients to a blender.
2. Blend on high speed until the mixture is smooth and creamy.
3. If the consistency is too thick, you can add a little more water and blend again.
4. Taste the smoothie and adjust the sweetness by adding a sweetener like honey or maple syrup if desired.
5. Pour the smoothie into two glasses and serve chilled.

STRAWBERRY LIME SMOOTHIE

This green smoothie combines the vibrant flavors of sweet basil, banana, and strawberries. Sesame seeds add a nutty taste and a source of healthy fats, while coconut water and ice create a refreshing and hydrating base. Sweet basil provides a unique twist and potential health benefits. The smoothie is packed with vitamins, minerals, and antioxidants from the fruits and herbs. It's a delicious and nutritious way to start your day or enjoy as a midday snack.

Calories: 160
Fat: 6 g
Carb: 27 g
Protein: 4 g
Fiber: 6 g
Time: 5 min
Servings: 2

Ingredients
- 1 1/2 oz. sweet basil
- 1 banana, peeled
- 3 oz. strawberries
- 1/2 lime, juiced
- 1 tbsp. sesame seeds
- 1 cup coconut water
- 1 cup ice

Instructions

1. Place all the ingredients in a blender.
2. Blend on high speed until the mixture is smooth and creamy.

FRESH PURPLE FIG SMOOTHIE

This green smoothie combines the natural sweetness of figs, grapes, and pear with the added nutritional boost of hemp seeds. Spinach adds a vibrant green color and is packed with vitamins and minerals. The smoothie is blended with water and ice to create a refreshing and hydrating base. It's a delicious way to incorporate fruits, veggies, and healthy fats into your diet. Enjoy this nutritious and flavorful green smoothie as a breakfast or snack option.

Calories: 160
Fat: 4 g
Carb: 30 g
Protein: 5 g
Fiber: 6 g
Time: 5 min
Servings: 2

Ingredients
- 1 fig
- 1 cup grapes
- 1 pear, chopped
- 1 tbsp. hemp seeds
- 1 cup water
- 1 cup ice
- Spinach (desired amount)

Instructions

1. Wash the spinach thoroughly and remove any tough stems.
2. Place the spinach, fig, grapes, pear, hemp seeds, water, and ice in a blender.
3. Blend on high speed until all the ingredients are well combined and the smoothie reaches a smooth consistency.
4. If the smoothie is too thick, you can add more water and blend again.
5. Taste the smoothie and adjust the sweetness by adding a sweetener like honey or maple syrup if desired.
6. Pour the smoothie into two glasses and serve chilled.

STRAWBERRY BEET SMOOTHIE

This green smoothie combines the earthy flavor of beets with the sweetness of strawberries and orange. The addition of lime juice and ginger adds a tangy and refreshing kick. Hemp seeds provide a source of plant-based protein and healthy fats. The smoothie is blended with water and ice for a smooth and creamy texture. Enjoy this vibrant and nutrient-rich green smoothie as a refreshing and energizing beverage.

Calories: 120
Fat: 4 g
Carb: 20 g
Protein: 4 g
Fiber: 5 g
Time: 5 min
Servings: 2

Ingredients
- 4 oz. Beets, scrubbed and chopped
- ¼ lbs. Strawberries
- 1 Orange, peeled
- 1 Lime, juiced
- ½ inch Ginger
- 1 tbsp. Hemp seeds
- 1 cup Water
- 1 cup Ice

Instructions
1. Peel and chop the beets, ensuring they are clean and free from any dirt.
2. Wash the strawberries and remove the stems.
3. Peel the orange and remove any seeds.
4. Juice the lime.
5. Peel and chop the ginger.
6. In a blender, combine the beets, strawberries, orange, lime juice, ginger, hemp seeds, water, and ice.
7. Blend on high speed until all the ingredients are well combined and the smoothie reaches a smooth consistency.
8. If the smoothie is too thick, you can add more water and blend again.
9. Taste the smoothie and adjust the sweetness by adding a natural sweetener like honey or maple syrup if desired.
10. Pour the smoothie into two glasses and serve chilled.

ZUCCHINI, WATERMELON AND COCONUT OIL SMOOTHIE

This green smoothie combines the fresh flavors of zucchini and watermelon. Zucchini adds a subtle vegetable taste, while watermelon provides a juicy and sweet element. The addition of coconut oil adds a hint of creaminess and healthy fat. The pinch of Himalayan pink salt enhances the overall flavor. Enjoy this light and hydrating green smoothie as a refreshing and nutritious beverage.

Calories: 170
Fat: 5 g
Carb: 8 g
Protein: 4 g
Fiber: 2 g
Time: 5 min
Servings: 2

Ingredients
- ½ cup chopped zucchini
- 1 cup seeded watermelon
- ½ teaspoon coconut oil
- a pinch of Himalayan pink salt

Instructions

1. Add all the ingredients to a blender.
2. Blend on high speed until the mixture is smooth and creamy.
3. If the consistency is too thick, you can add a little more water and blend again.
4. Taste the smoothie and adjust the sweetness by adding a sweetener like honey or maple syrup if desired.
5. Pour the smoothie into two glasses and serve chilled.

CUCUMBER, PLAME AND CUMIN SMOOTHIE

This green smoothie combines the refreshing flavors of cucumber and plum. The addition of cumin powder adds a subtle and unique twist, while the lime juice provides a tangy kick. The pinch of Himalayan pink salt enhances the overall flavor profile. Enjoy this hydrating and flavorful green smoothie as a nutritious and energizing beverage.

Calories: 160
Fat: 1 g
Carb: 25 g
Protein: 4 g
Fiber: 3 g
Time: 5 min
Servings: 2

Ingredients
- 2 cups cucumber
- ½ cup plum
- 1 tsp. cumin powder
- 1 tbsp. lime juice
- a pinch of Himalayan pink salt

Instructions

1. Peel and chop the cucumber into smaller pieces.
2. Remove the pit from the plum and cut it into chunks.
3. In a blender, add the chopped cucumber, plum chunks, cumin powder, lime juice, and a pinch of Himalayan pink salt.
4. Blend on high speed until all the ingredients are well combined and the smoothie reaches a smooth consistency.
5. If the smoothie is too thick, you can add a splash of water or coconut water to adjust the consistency.
6. Taste the smoothie and adjust the flavors by adding more lime juice or salt if needed.
7. Pour the smoothie into two glasses and serve chilled.

LEAVES OF THE AMARANTH, STRAWBERRY AND SWEET BASIL SMOOTHIE

This green smoothie combines the nutritious amaranth leaves with the sweetness of strawberries and the aromatic flavor of sweet basil. The addition of coconut water not only adds hydration but also brings a tropical touch to the smoothie. Enjoy this refreshing and nutrient-packed green smoothie as a healthy beverage option.

Calories: 150
Fat: 1 g
Carb: 25 g
Protein: 3 g
Fiber: 3 g
Time: 5 min
Servings: 2

Ingredients
- 1 oz. blackberries
- 4 oz. apple
- 1 pear, chopped
- 3 basil leaves
- 3 tbsp. cashews
- 1 cup water
- 1 cup ice

Instructions

1. Wash the amaranth leaves thoroughly and remove any tough stems.
2. Chop the strawberries into smaller pieces.
3. In a blender, combine the amaranth leaves, chopped strawberries, sweet basil, and coconut water.
4. Blend on high speed until all the ingredients are well blended and the smoothie reaches a smooth consistency.
5. If the smoothie is too thick, you can add more coconut water to adjust the consistency.
6. Pour the smoothie into two glasses and serve immediately.

MAIN INGREDIENTS USED AND ITS BENEFITS

Spinach: is a superfood that packs a punch of nutrients when added to smoothies. It is low in calories but high in fiber, vitamins A and C, iron, and calcium. Adding spinach to your smoothies can help boost your immune system, improve digestion, and promote healthy skin, hair, and bones.

Kale: is a nutrient-packed leafy green that is an excellent addition to smoothies. It's high in vitamins A, C, and K, and is a good source of fiber and calcium. Adding kale to your smoothies is a delicious way to boost your nutrient intake and support overall health.

Celery: is a nutrient-dense vegetable that is a great addition to any smoothie. It is low in calories and high in fiber, which helps support healthy digestion. Celery is also rich in vitamins and minerals, including vitamin K, vitamin C, potassium, and folate, making it a healthy choice for any smoothie recipe.

Banana: They blend beautifully into nearly any recipe and provide a sweetness and creaminess that compliments the savory flavor of greens. Plus, they're full of potassium, which wards against cramps and helps lower blood pressure.

Collard Greens: It helps to keep bones strong and healthy — a plus for a lot of women. Many people think taking a calcium supplement is the only way to keep their bones strong, but a few cups of collard greens a week is a huge help!

Chia Seeds: Chia seeds are among the healthiest foods in the world. These tiny seeds are loaded with nutrients proven to energize, satiate, and even aid in weight loss. Plus, chia seeds have virtually zero taste, which makes them an ideal addition to almost any smoothie.

Apricot: Apricots are a good source of catechins, a family of flavonoid phytonutrients. These small fruits contain four to five grams of the anti-inflammatory catechins, as well as vitamins A and C.

Avocados: Not only do they provide your body with the good kind of fat (fat that keeps your metabolism revved up), they also tell your body's fat storage hormones to turn off, making it more difficult for fat cells to actually build up.

Cinnamon: While cinnamon doesn't exactly boost your metabolism by itself, it does help fat cells respond better to insulin, which aids in sugar being processed more efficiently in your body. An efficient sugar process means more energy, less stored fat!

Pineapple, Oranges: These are the foods which are high in Vitamin C. Vitamin C is crucial to the production of carnitine, a molecule that helps your muscles get their energy from fat. A study was even published in the *Journal of Nutrition* that found "people with higher levels of C in their blood had lower BMIs and less body fat."

Whey Protein: High-quality whey protein is a pretty important component when you're trying to lose weight. When you're shedding fat via a diet or exercise regime, you want to make sure you're not shedding muscle along with it and supplementing your diet with a smoothie full of whey (or another high-quality protein) keeps your muscles full and your metabolism working at full speed.

Zucchini: Zucchini has a good amount of lutein and zeaxanthin, phytonutrients that promote healthy eyesight. If you want a side dish that has a lot of health benefits but not a lot of calories, then zucchini is for you. Coming in at only 21 calories a cup, you can add some spices, salt and pepper, and saute yourself a satisfying, low-calorie side.

Carrots: With an abundance of vitamins A, C, K, E, beta-carotene, fiber, potassium, folate, manganese, and antioxidants, carrots have never been more appealing!

Grapefruit: Grapefruit's dense peel helps keep pesticides away from the juicy fruit. This is another reason why you can indulge on this low-sugar, vitamin C filled treat without an ounce of guilt.

Mango: This rich and creamy fruit is another one that can be eaten without worry thanks to its thick peel that protects its insides from toxic chemicals.

Papayas: This exotic fruit is rich in vitamins A, B, E, and K, as well as vital antioxidants.

Cantaloupe: Cantaloupes have thick outer skins; therefore, their juicy insides are protected from harmful pesticides.

Matcha: Matcha is also full of catechins and antioxidants that have been shown to help fight against, and possibly even prevent, cancer.

Ginger: It will help that nauseous feeling go away. It soothes sore muscles, improves circulation, and could even ward off certain cancers.

Beets: They help your blood and brain fight degenerative diseases and also improve your performance at the gym.

Strawberries: A fat free and low calorie food, strawberries are full of fiber. They're also full of polyphenols, antioxidants that have been specifically categorized as cancer fighters (red wine and green tea have them too). Eight regular-sized strawberries will give you almost a full day's worth of vitamin C, and eating strawberries may also help in removing surface stains and plaque from teeth.

CONCLUSION

In conclusion, green smoothies are a delicious and easy way to boost your health and incorporate more nutrient-dense foods into your diet. By blending together fruits, vegetables, and other superfoods, you can create a tasty and satisfying meal or snack that will leave you feeling energized and refreshed.

Through this book of green smoothie recipes, we have explored a variety of flavor combinations and ingredient options to help you discover your new favorite smoothie. From classic green smoothies to tropical and fruity blends, there is something for everyone in this book.

Not only are green smoothies a great way to increase your intake of essential vitamins and minerals, but they are also an excellent source of fiber, which can aid in digestion and weight management. And by using whole foods instead of processed ingredients, you can feel good about what you are putting into your body.

Remember, there are no strict rules when it comes to making green smoothies. Experiment with different ingredients and ratios to find what works best for you. And don't be afraid to get creative and add in your own favorite superfoods or supplements.

By incorporating green smoothies into your daily routine, you can improve your overall health and wellbeing while enjoying delicious and satisfying meals. So grab your blender, stock up on some fresh produce, and start blending your way to a healthier you!